THE MANUAL OF
NUDE PHOTOGRAPHY

THE MANUAL OF
NUDE PHOTOGRAPHY

JON GRAY text by MICHAEL BUSSELLE

SPHERE BOOKS LIMITED
30-32 Gray's Inn Road, London WC1X 8JL

First published in Great
Britain in hardback by
Sphere Books Ltd 1983

Copyright © 1983 Robert
Adkinson Limited
Published in paperback
by Sphere Books Ltd 1984

SPHERE

ISBN 0 7221 2111 3

Designed and produced
by Robert Adkinson
Limited, London

Editorial Director
Clare Howell

Editor
Hilary Dickinson

Art Editor
Christopher White

Designer
Roy Williams

Design Assistant
Jane Morey

Illustrations
Rick Blakely

Text set in Itek Helvetica
light 8½ on 11 pt by
Hugh Wilson Typesetting,
Norwich
Illustrations originated by
East Anglian Engraving
Ltd, Norwich
Printed and bound in Italy
by L.E.G.O. Vicenza

Reprinted 1984

CONTENTS

FIRST
SESSIONS

WHAT IS NUDE PHOTOGRAPHY?

There are a great many approaches to nude photography – it is in many ways one of the more subjective styles of photography – and there is probably a greater polarization between the attitudes towards the way it is done and the way it is seen than there is with other subjects. The sexual connotations of the nude are also stronger in photography than in other art mediums. This may well be because the more 'realistic' qualities of a photograph make it easier for the viewer to identify a photographic image more closely with a real person than a statue or a painting allows, but whatever the reason, nude photography is undoubtedly most widely used in the more personal and sexual way.

The 'pin-up' approach is in many ways the most basic style of nude photography, in which the personality and sexuality of the model form an important element of the image, and much of the photographer's skill is directed towards distilling these elusive elements into a form that can be recorded on film. This approach was initiated in the Victorian era in the form of postcards, evolved and matured in the heyday of Hollywood, and is alive and well today in the medium of the pin-ups in popular newspapers and the 'girlie' magazines. Today, many pictures of this type are very explicit and their acceptability in terms of taste can often be questionable. As a consequence, a style of photography has evolved in which the erotic and sexual nature of the image is made more acceptable by the use of more calculated and contrived photographic techniques to create a degree of mood or ambiguity. Whereas the photographic techniques and aesthetic approach to the basic pin-up picture are very simple and direct, the more atmospheric pictures of photographers such as David Hamilton, Sam Haskins, and Helmut Newton are far more complex in both conception and execution. This style of photography uses the model both as an individual and simply as an element in a composition in which the setting or location plays an equally dominant role.

A further extension of this approach is completely to lose or hide the identity of the model so that her body simply becomes a visual element in the image. In this way the picture becomes an abstraction rather than a photograph of a particular person. This can be achieved in a variety of ways, for example by asking the model simply to turn her head away from the camera. This device alone can have a quite strong, depersonalizing effect, in contrast to the pin-up type picture where the model's eyes are invariably directed into the camera inviting the viewer to acknowledge her as an individual. However, the more anonymous quality of such pictures need not mean any loss in erotic effect – in fact, there can even be an element of voyeurism in which an intimate and personal moment is briefly revealed, and this can in some instances create a heightened, if less obvious, sense of eroticism. Another way of creating a more abstract image is to move in much closer and to frame the picture much more tightly so that only small parts of the body are included. This approach

can be used to produce pictures which are almost totally abstract in which the model herself is no longer an important element, and it is simply the tones and shapes created by the contours of her body and the lighting which are recorded on the film. This type of nude photography has a considerable affinity with landscape work, and techniques which emphasize the elements of texture and form, for instance, are of equal importance in both fields.

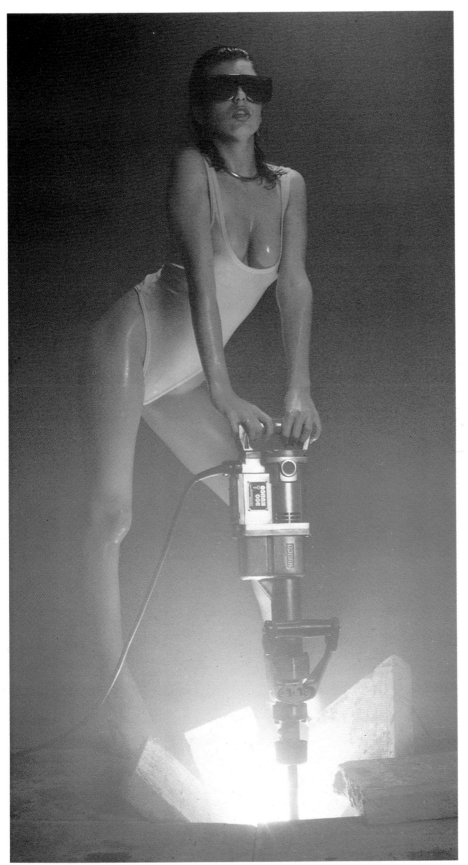

There are many types and styles of nude photography, ranging from the abstract (**opposite above**), to the pin-up (**opposite below**), the contrived (**left**) and the atmospheric (**below**).

EXOTIC/GLAMOUR 1

The effect of any photograph depends equally on the style of the model and on the approach of the photographer. This is particularly true of nude photography, which offers scope for many imaginative images.

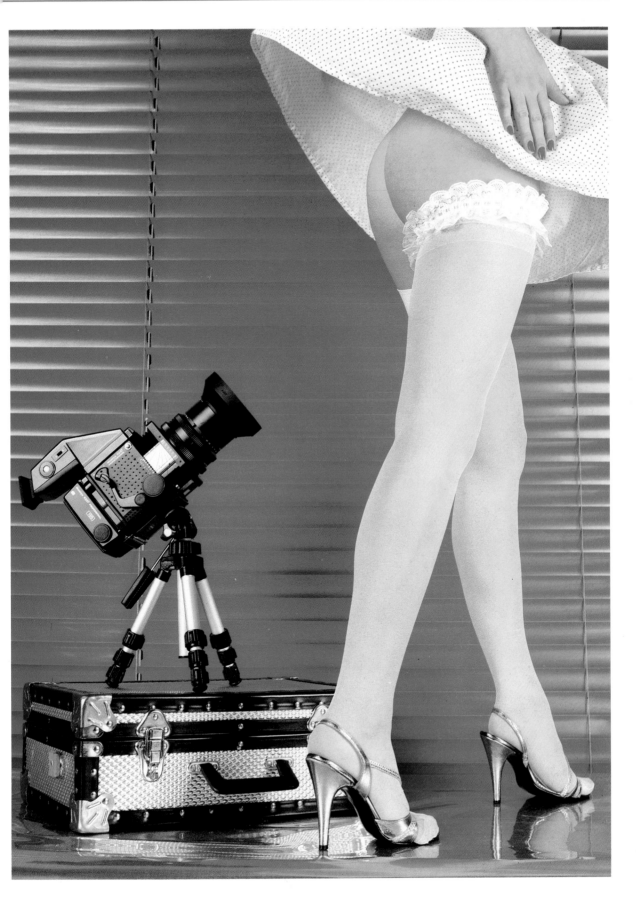

EXOTIC/GLAMOUR 2

These three pictures illustrate
the versatility of the nude
medium: a glamorous bedroom
shot (**opposite**), a more overt
'pin-up' picture (**left**) and an
exotic jungle setting (**below**).

EXOTIC/GLAMOUR 3

An imaginative choice of both setting and props has produced widely contrasting styles, from the bizarre to the jokey to the titillating.

FULL BODY/PARTS OF BODY 1

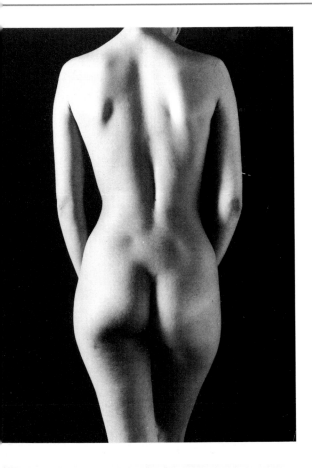

By careful framing of individual
parts of the body, it is possible
to create a great variety of
effective abstract images.

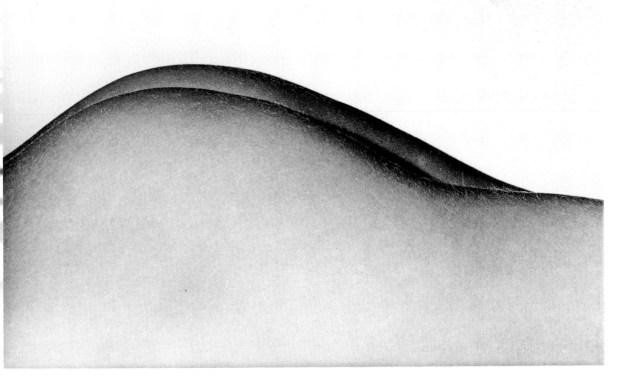

FULL BODY/PARTS OF BODY 2

*The use of a thin fabric screen, both in front of and behind the model, has added interest to the simple nude body shot (**below**). By contrast, an altogether more erotic effect has been created by the surprising juxtaposition of the savage dog against the white-stockinged legs of the model (**opposite**).*

MALE NUDE 1

Although the male nude has been featured quite promin-ently in classical and traditional art it is seldom used as a subject in photography. This may be because the majority of photographers are men and they quite simply find more pleasure in photographing women, or it is perhaps more likely that the commercial applications of the male nude are far more restricted. From a purely visual point of view, however, there is no reason why this should be so, particularly when the prime purpose is merely to create pleasing images, since the more muscular and sinewy contours of a man's body can in some circumstances be photographed even more effectively than the softer, more bland quality of a woman's form.

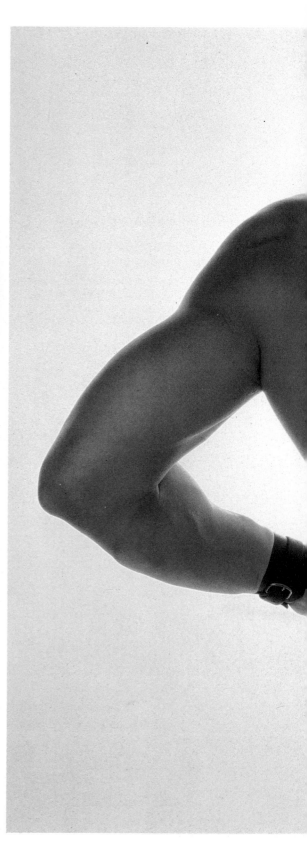

*The tough, latently aggressive figure against the stark red background (**above**) stands in marked contrast to the abstract nude where the outline of the model's body is thrown into relief by the back-lighting (**right**).*

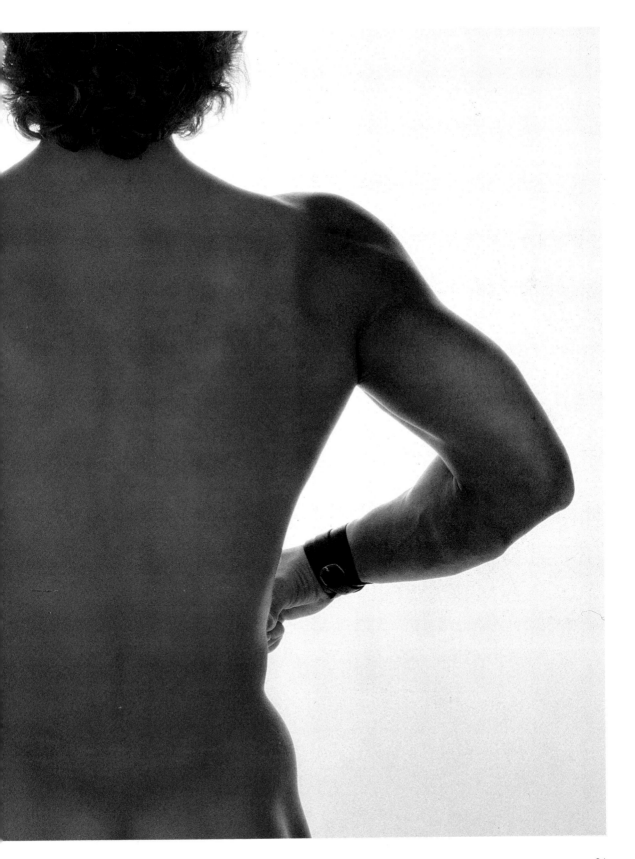

MALE NUDE 2

*The qualities of the male nude figure can be exploited just as readily as those of the female nude to produce strong and varied photographic images. In these three pictures, slight variations in the model's pose have created in turn a feeling of aloofness, reflection and strength (**below left and right, opposite**). In every case, the lighting emphasizes the muscular contours of the model's body.*

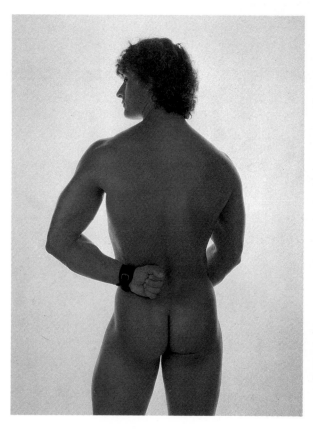

HOME STUDIO

The first attempt at taking any unfamiliar type of photograph is almost certainly likely to throw up a few problems or difficulties that have not been anticipated. Nude photography may well prove to be more prone to this than other types of picture, simply because in addition to the usual technical and aesthetic factors there is the all-important consideration of creating and maintaining a good rapport with the model. This can be much more difficult to achieve when there is a degree of uncertainty or unfamiliarity on the part of the photographer, and doubly so if the model is also inexperienced. For this reason the inexperienced amateur photographer embarking on a first session may find it beneficial to work with a professional model who will be able to make a more positive contribution to the pictures. If this is not possible then it would at least be helpful to ask a close friend to act as model for the first session since this will at least ensure that there is a relaxed atmosphere and some of the pressure will be diffused.

In most cases the session will probably take place in a studio of some sort, whether it is a fully equipped professional studio or a makeshift home studio. This is in fact a good choice as the studio environment offers comfort and privacy, both of which are important in creating a relaxed and productive working atmosphere, while the degree of control over lighting, backgrounds, and props can also be helpful. Whichever type of studio is used it is important to be well prepared. If you are setting up a studio in your home, for example, do so well in advance of the session, making sure that all the equipment is working and that you have spare lamps where necessary and that everything you will need is to hand. It can also be useful, with a friend as a substitute for a model, to set up your lighting and check exposure levels, particularly if you do not use the equipment very often.

If you are planning a session in a home studio, it is sensible to set up and check all the equipment beforehand, and to familiarize yourself with the setting.

PROFESSIONAL STUDIO

If you are using a hired studio ask if you can go there a day or so beforehand just to familiarize yourself with the equipment and to make sure that there are no additional accessories that you will want to take along. Even more important than preparing the equipment, make sure that you yourself are prepared in terms of ideas for shots. The main difficulty with studio photography is that you simply cannot afford to hope that something will evolve as you go along – a studio shot can only consist of what *you* put into it, and unless you have thought your shot through and made sure that you have the necessary props and backgrounds and that the model brings along the right clothes and accessories then the results will invariably be dull and disappointing. This can obviously be disastrous, especially if you are committed to paying model fees. The professional nude photographer cannot allow this to happen, and it is a good idea as an amateur to adopt the basic methods of organizing and shooting a session that are used in a professional studio.

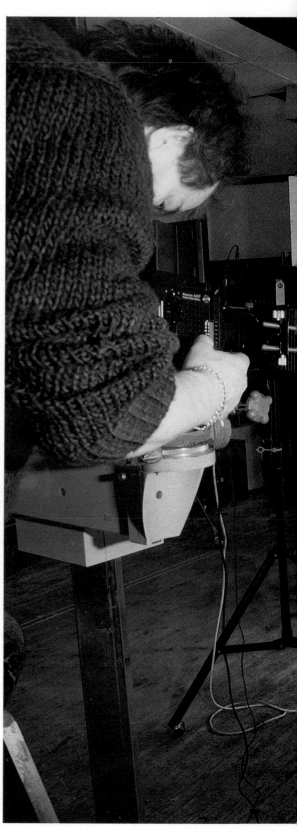

A session in a professional studio must be planned and prepared with care if the outcome is to be successful and unnecessary time and expense spared.

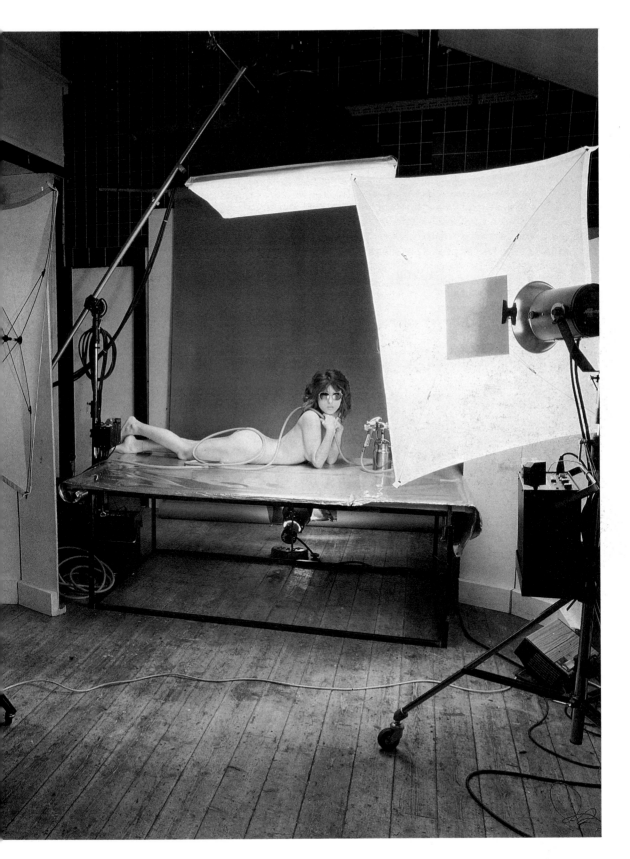

PREPARATION AND PLANNING

When you have selected a model and arranged the basic studio facilities the next thing is to sketch out some rough ideas or visuals for your pictures. These do not necessarily have to be followed rigidly once the session is under-way but it is important to have a definite starting-point and a firm idea of what sort of picture you want to finish up with. At this stage it is worth while involving your model as she may well have some ideas about what she could contribute to the pictures: for example, she may have clothes or accessories that could create just the right atmosphere, or she may be able to arrange her hair or make-up to fit a particular theme. But in any case it is important that you should be able to communicate both your ideas and your enthusiasm in order for her to be able to work effectively. The next thing is to make a list of items you may need for props and for any special background effects. Most professional studios have a props cupboard full of bits and pieces that can be used to add the finishing touch to a shot, as well as a wide variety of background colours and fabrics. It is, however, unlikely that these resources will be available to most amateurs so this should be thought about beforehand. In addition to planning the basic ideas and props for a session it is also worth considering whether any particular photographic or lighting techniques could make a useful contribution – soft focus attachments, for instance, or effects filters. You might want to hire a special piece of equipment to create a particular effect, such as a spotlight or a wind machine; most professional dealers stock a wide range of this type of accessory that can be hired for just a day.

Last but not least, remember your model's creature comforts: make sure there is a suitable place where she can change and do her hair and make-up, and that it is equipped with a good mirror and adequate lighting. Have coffee or a drink available, particularly if it is going to be a long session. Make sure the studio is really warm as cold conditions can be a very negative factor in nude photography and can ruin a session. It is also a good idea to have some background music as this can help to create a relaxed atmosphere.

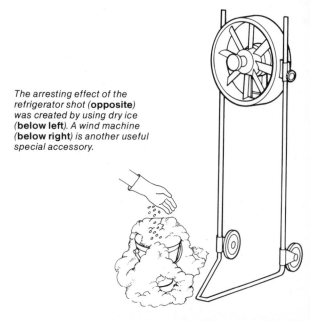

The arresting effect of the refrigerator shot (**opposite**) *was created by using dry ice* (**below left**). *A wind machine* (**below right**) *is another useful special accessory.*

FINDING A MODEL

Whatever else you may need for nude photography one thing is certain – you need a model. The right model can in fact make all the difference between a simply good picture and an outstanding one, while the wrong model can make it impossible to produce a good picture from the very best ideas even if everything else is perfect. Finding the right model can be a major stumbling block particularly for the amateur who may not be able to afford the fees of a good professional model. This is not to suggest that it is not possible to take good pictures of amateur models, rather the main point is that in order to find a suitable professional model all you need do is look through the model directories and pick up the telephone, while finding an amateur model can be much less straightforward.

The essential difference between a professional model and an amateur is that the former has had more experience and has learnt some of the tricks of the trade: a good professional model, for example, usually has a good idea of how she looks in the camera and will know instinctively how to move and pose without the need for constant direction, and she will have learnt how to adapt her make-up and hair-style in the most effective way. On the other hand, this experience can have drawbacks and in some situations the rather glossy, stylized look of a professional model can appear out of place and can actually detract from a picture unless she is given the right sort of direction. Another advantage of working with a professional model is that she will have accumulated a suitable wardrobe of clothes and accessories and will also know how to make the best use of them.

If you are looking for a professional model through an agency, they will send you index cards of the models on their list. The card contains a selection of pictures of the model, and gives her vital statistics and other relevant personal details.

PLANOGRAPHIC INDEX CARDS (1982) 01 769 6111

John Pickering

Chris Thompson

Eric Swayne

QUALITIES IN A MODEL

In nude work, the personality of the model is equally as important as her appearance, and in certain respects even more so. When planning a session, it is vital to consider the model's attitude, as she may well have definite feelings about certain types of shot. While one girl may be quite uninhibited about posing for a completely nude picture, another may prefer to do topless shots. In the same way, a particular model may be ideal for a titillating, overtly erotic sequence, and another more suitable for abstract studies.

DIFFERENT TYPES OF MODEL

Every model has her own style, and a girl who is confident and relaxed will be able to project her personality to create a strongly individual image.

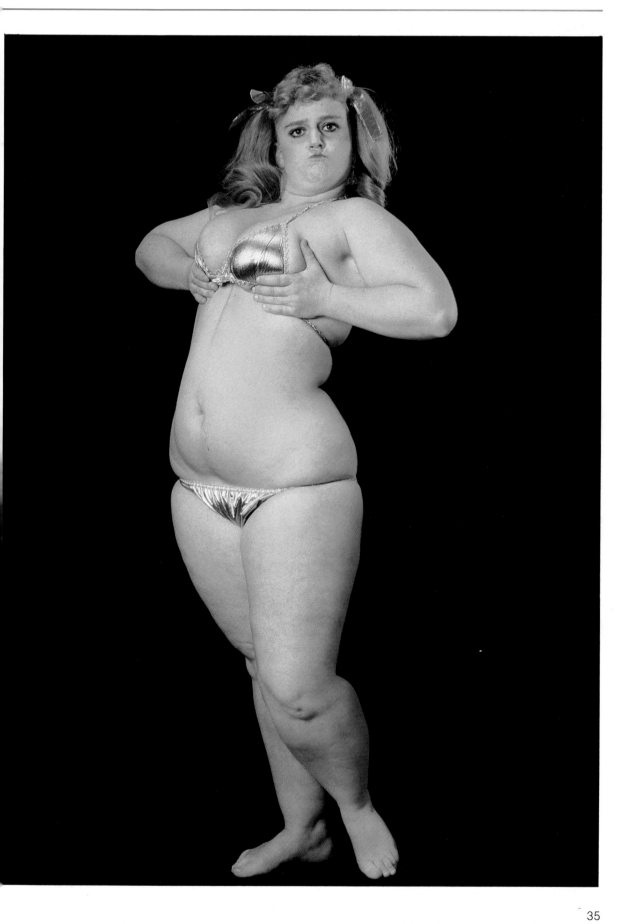

PROFESSIONAL MODEL

The best and easiest way to book a professional model is through a model agency. These can be located through the local telephone directory or in the specialized media reference books. It is important to appreciate, however, that by no means all models or indeed all model agencies are prepared to do nude work and you should establish this before you approach them. Once you have contacted an agency they will send you index cards from which to make a selection. This is a printed card, usually A5 size (approx. 6 x 8 in), single or folded, with a selection of pictures of the particular model printed in black-and-white and colour; it will also include details of her vital statistics and of any special skills or features such as good hands or legs or the ability to dance. In some instances it is possible to go to the model agency and interview some of the models you would like to consider – this obviously has the advantage that you can make a more objective decision about their potential and you will be able to look through their portfolios which will provide a much wider range of pictures than the index cards. If the booking is likely to be for a day or more, or if it is for an important assignment such as a magazine feature or a calendar, then the agency will arrange a casting session for your short-list of models so that they can visit your studio or office with their portfolios and perhaps do some test shots.

If you have established a working relationship with a particular agency or if you can approach one with a good portfolio of your own work then it is possible on occasion to arrange test sessions with models who want pictures for their own portfolios or index cards. This is often a good opportunity for both the model and the photographer to do experimental work and try out new ideas, though these pictures would not be used for publication unless a specific agreement was reached with the model. Where pictures are intended for publication it is important to make this quite clear to the model and to obtain her signature on a model release form. This is simply a formal agreement allowing the pictures to be published, and blank forms can be obtained from a variety of sources such as the Bureau of Freelance Photographers in Britain or the ASMP (Association of Magazine Photographers) in the United States.

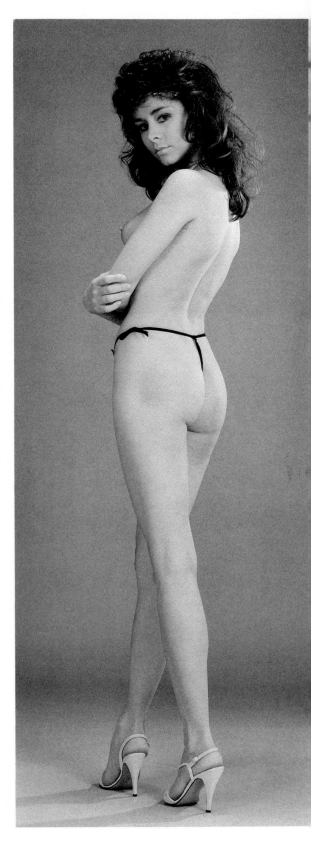

As a result of practice and experience, a professional model will have learnt how to move and pose in a natural and relaxed way without the need for too much direction by the photographer. All models also have their own stock of make-up and accessories which they can use to add interest to a session.

AMATEUR MODEL

Finding an amateur model is largely a question of exploiting your friends and suitable contacts, while semi-professional models can be found in amateur studio clubs and sometimes art schools will provide a list of models who pose for the life classes. It does take some measure of courage simply to approach a stranger on the street or standing at a bus stop, but this is in fact how many professional photographers manage to keep finding new models. If you decide to try this approach you should adopt a strictly professional manner and not attempt it if you are likely to be at all embarrassed or inarticulate. First of all, present a business card and explain briefly the sort of work you do and how you feel she might be able to help, then just leave her to consider it and ask her to telephone you if she is interested.

You may find that one of your friends or acquaintances is willing to model for a nude session. As an amateur model has not acquired the experience in posing and creating an interesting image that a professional model has, it is best to keep the shots simple until she has gained more confidence.

PUTTING THE MODEL AT HER EASE

Whether you engage a professional or an amateur model it is important in all cases that you are able to put the model at her ease and make her feel quite confident that your pictures will do her credit. The best way to achieve this is to have a good portfolio of your work which you can show her. Most people feel rather vulnerable in front of a camera especially when being photographed nude, and even an experienced professional can feel awkward and ill-at-ease if she feels that you are not competent. This is another reason for ensuring that the studio is well pre-pared and that you have a well-developed and firm idea of what you are trying to achieve.

If a photographic session is to be successful, there has to be a good rapport between the photographer and the model to enable them to work well together. The photographer should explain what sort of atmosphere he is trying to evoke, and the sort of poses he wants her to adopt, as this will help the model to relate to the mood and feel relaxed.

HOW A PROFESSIONAL PHOTOGRAPHER WORKS 1

The work of a professional photographer falls into three main categories. The first is an assignment in which he is briefed and paid by a client to produce a particular picture or series of pictures to fit a specific layout or theme, such as a calendar. The second is the speculative session for which he is not commissioned but takes pictures at his own expense for a specific market such as a particular magazine or a calendar publisher or possibly for a picture library to which he regularly supplies photographs. The third category is the more personally motivated work, which may simply be for his own pleasure or to add new material to his portfolio. This last category most closely resembles the way in which the majority of amateur photographers tend to work in so far as the pictures are not directly related to earning fees and consequently there is much greater freedom in both the type of pictures taken and the approach which is adopted. Nevertheless neither the professional nor the serious amateur will allow such sessions to become aimless: the success of the pictures will inevitably be the result of a well-planned session coupled with good ideas even if greater flexibility is possible in the course of shooting than would be possible when working to a client's brief. One of the most significant aspects of this type of picture is that the photographer has a completely free hand in his choice of model whereas when a picture is being taken for an assignment or for a specific market this choice will obviously be much more restricted.

The selection of a model is often something over which the photographer has only a limited degree of control when a large or important assignment is being planned, such as a calendar or a magazine spread, and several people may be involved in the choice, with the client or art director having the casting vote. However, the photographer's own preferences and recommendations will also be important since personality and compatibility are important factors especially when a trip is planned. The first step in such an assignment will be the initial approach to a particular photographer; at this stage the client will usually be considering several possible photographers for the job and each will be asked to take along his portfolio and possibly to discuss ideas and approaches to the photography as well as availability and of course fees. This is why a portfolio is so important to a professional photographer and he will make sure that it is frequently updated, both with pictures taken specially for the purpose, perhaps of a more experimental or innovative nature, and with recently published work. Once the photographer has been selected, the next step will usually be a meeting with the art director and possibly the client to discuss where, when and how the pictures will be taken. If the job is a calendar or advertising for a national account, the agency or design group will almost certainly have already submitted layouts to the client, usually done as Pentel roughs or sketches indicating the basic ideas and theme of the session; there might be several roughs and the client will select the one he feels most appropriate to the product. If a photographer has already been engaged, he will usually be invited to make comments and suggestions even if only to indicate what may or may not be possible, as some visuals can be rather impractical.

At this stage it is quite likely that the location will have been decided; this may be a tie-up with perhaps an airline or travel company who will offer concessions on fares and accommodation in exchange for being credited in the publication. Although major national accounts usually have

Every photographic session on location presents its own problems. For a street scene, for example, there is the immediate difficulty of finding an area free of both traffic and unwanted onlookers.

For a trip which involves more than one model it is likely that different types of girl will be chosen, such as a brunette and a fair-skinned blond, to provide more variety and flexibility for the photographer.

If the photographer has been commissioned for an assignment by a large company, his freedom of choice of both the model and the location may be somewhat restricted, although his views and recommendations will also be important to ensure a successful outcome.

HOW A PROFESSIONAL PHOTOGRAPHER WORKS 2

quite large photographic budgets the expenses of such a trip can be high and ways of reducing the costs are always considered. If the chosen location is not one that either the photographer or art director, or both, is familiar with it is likely that a reconnaissance trip will be made to look for settings and backgrounds and to organize any special facilities well in advance. This may be done quite separately some months ahead or the photographer and art director may travel out a few days before the models arrive.

Once the location and the date of the trip have been fixed, the next thing will be to choose a model. The first step is to go through the index cards and model books and make a preliminary list of possible candidates. At this stage the model's availability will be a deciding factor since although trips are planned months ahead there tends to be a 'season' for this type of work and many trips are often planned at the same period of the year. The first selection of suitable models who are available will be invited to attend a casting session either at the offices of the agency or at the photographer's studio. They will be asked to bring their portfolios and possibly to be prepared to do a test shot on Polaroid for reference. There are likely to be several people present at the casting session – including the photographer, art director, account executive and the client – and for an important account several days and sessions can be involved before a final short list is drawn up. Until the final decision is made, all the models under consideration will be provisionally booked to ensure that someone else does not snap them up. If two, three or more models are involved on a trip it is likely that they will be chosen with variety in mind: a dark-haired girl with a blond perhaps, or one with a slim, boyish figure to contrast with a more voluptuous model. As well as the models, art director, photographer and client there is also likely to be a photographer's assistant, a make-up artist and possibly a stylist on the trip; the stylist is responsible for arranging and organizing all the props, accessories and wardrobe as well as helping to set up shots and arrange settings.

It is vital to the success of any trip that the model and photographer get on well together to produce a relaxed working atmosphere.

STAGE-BY-STAGE 1

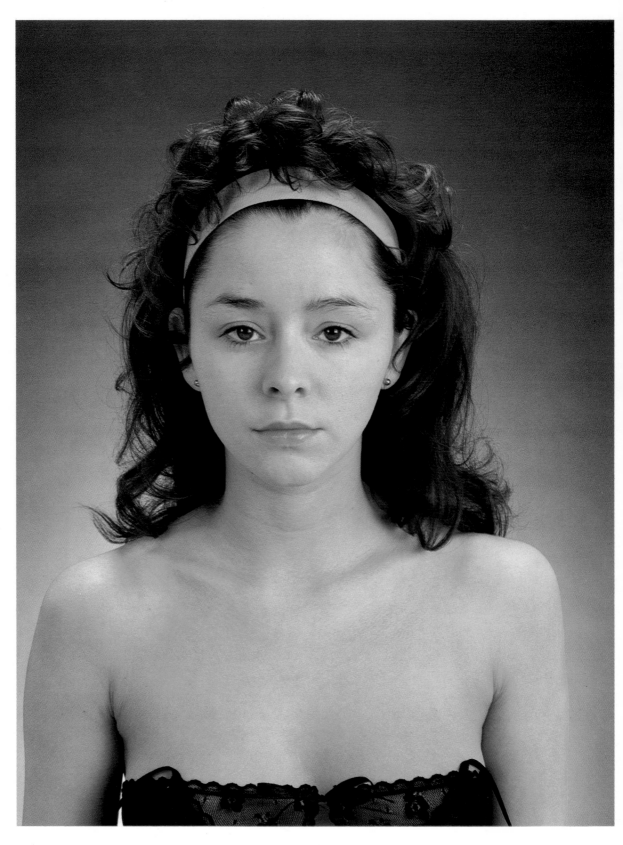

Make-up is an important part of the preparations for a photograph, both to mask any skin blemishes and minimize shine or texture, and to emphasize particular facial features (**opposite**).

The main stages consist of the application of tinted foundation to disguise blemishes, matt powder to remove shine, blusher to highlight the cheek-bones and eye shadow and eye liner to emphasize the eye area.

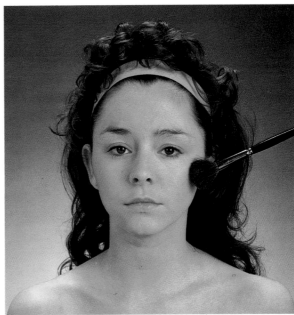

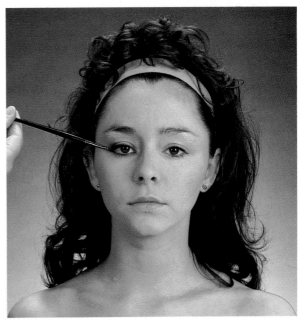

STAGE-BY-STAGE 2

The last stages of a full make-up are the application of mascara and lip gloss.

The final result, with the model fully made up and her hair dressed, has added life and sparkle to her whole appearance.

BODY MAKE-UP

In nude photography, make-up is used not only on the face, but also on the body. In addition to its role of hiding blemishes it can be used to create exaggerated, even weird, effects.

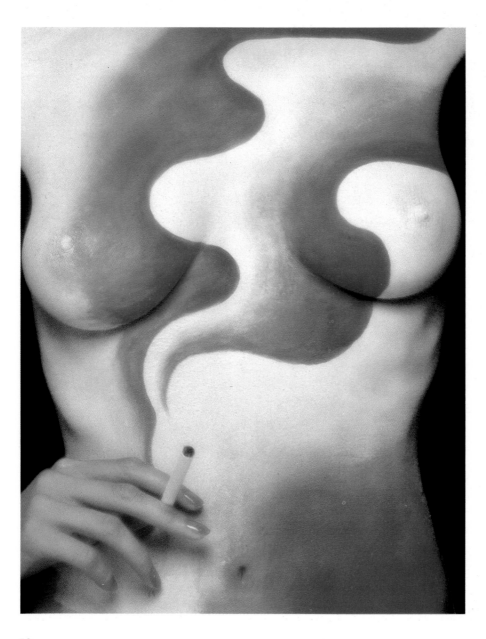

EXOTIC MAKE-UP

The over-all effect of a picture is influenced by the style of make-up which is chosen. In these three examples, the sophisticated make-up, accentuating the model's lips and eyes, and the choice of suitable accessories, underlines the glamorous mood.

CREATIVE CHOICE 1

The background of a picture often plays a very minor role in nude photography, but this is certainly not always the case and, indeed, this aspect of a shot can be very important, particularly where it is necessary to create additional interest or atmosphere. The stock background available in most studios consists of the large rolls of coloured cartridge paper supplied by professional dealers. While much can be done to create quite interesting effects with lighting on this background, its use is quite limited, and the model will also find it less conducive to producing relaxed and natural poses. A proper set or setting, on the other hand, can give her the stimulus to become more involved in the mood of a picture.

There are essentially three approaches to using settings in photography: to design and construct a setting, to find an existing setting, or to use a combination of both methods. In many cases the actual area of a set needed for a nude picture is quite small, particularly if it is not a full-length shot, and the task of constructing a suitable set is not actually as daunting as it may seem. A great deal can be achieved with the aid of two or three wall flats – wooden frames about 8 x 4 feet (2.4 x 1.2 metres) covered in hardboard, masonite, or plywood – which can be clamped together to create a variety of shapes and angles and can be either painted or covered in wallpaper or fabric. It is worth bearing in mind that really quite crude construc-

tions can be adequate since the camera will see only a restricted view of the set and in any case it is not the main feature of the picture and will often not be completely sharp. The flexibility of this type of setting can be greatly increased by the addition of a few props such as a window frame or door and some pieces of furniture (a visit to a junk shop or a demolition site can often provide a useful stock of items of this sort).

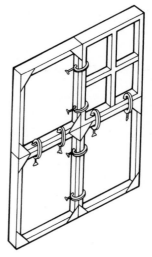

*Additional interest can be given to a shot by the choice of background. It can be a white background paper, which will form an effective contrast to a prop such as a chair (**below left**); a coloured blanket on which the model can lie (**far right**); or the model can be positioned behind a plastic screen (**right**). To provide more scope, a simple indoor setting can be constructed from a series of wall flats and window frames (**below**).*

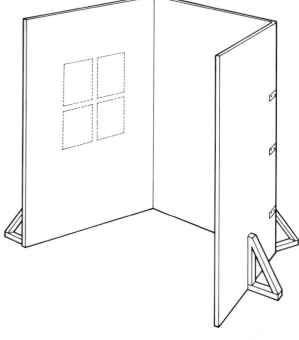

CREATIVE CHOICE 2

The two exotic nude studies illustrate the creative possibilities of the studio setting shown above.

INDOOR SETTINGS

Looking for a ready-made setting will obviously be both less costly and less time-consuming, and most photographers who do this type of work regularly will always be thinking in terms of future sessions when they are out and about. With an indoor setting the main thing to look for is space and flexibility – for example, it is not a good idea to use settings that are too cluttered or fussily decorated since it is much easier to add the odd piece of furniture or a prop to dress it up rather than be restricted in the choice of viewpoints and the framing of shots to avoid distracting backgrounds. Unless you are looking for a setting for one specific shot it is always best to view a potential location in terms of how many possible angles and corners can be used: it is easy to get carried away with an impressive interior only to find that when you start to work there is essentially only one viewpoint, particularly if you had planned a lengthy session. If you are intending to shoot with available light then this too will be an important consideration; look at the position of the windows to see how restricting they might be to your pictures, and even if you plan to use portable lighting equipment it is always worth considering the ways in which existing light can be used in an attractive interior in order to create atmosphere even if you supplement it. Remember to check the availability of power points and make sure you have the right plugs and extension leads if necessary. As space is an important consideration, particularly if you intend to shoot full-length pictures, it is worth taking along a camera with a standard lens when you do a reconnaissance as a deceptively long 'throw' may be needed; ceiling height can also be a problem in such circumstances. If it is an important session – for an assignment perhaps or involving model fees – then it is worth while shooting a few Polaroids of the setting you plan to use from different angles, as this will enable you to anticipate any problems or restrictions that may be encountered later.

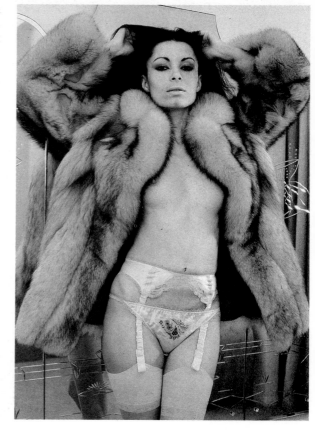

An indoor setting can range from the very simple, such as a mirrored wall of a room, to a window shot which offers varied lighting effects, to a wider view which takes in interesting angles and corners.

OUTDOOR SETTINGS

The same basic criteria which govern indoor settings apply to outside locations: look for a variety of possible backgrounds and angles within a particular location and also make a note of the angle and direction of the sunlight at different times of the day and how this might affect your shooting schedule. As with interior locations, do not necessarily go for an impressive view. It is invariably the small corners and details of a scene that will be useful to your pictures and often the best locations are places that might not merit a second glance from the purely scenic point of view. With outdoor settings there are two other important considerations: access and privacy. Ideally you want somewhere that you can get close to by car as even a few hundred yards can be a nuisance when carrying camera equipment and model bags. The car will often be the most suitable and convenient base from which to work, it will provide somewhere for the model to change and make up, as well as being a convenient place to leave equipment and clothes which are not being used.

Privacy is particularly important for nude photography, not only because it might cause offence to some people or even break the law, but because the presence, or even threat, of intruders and onlookers can create a serious distraction and inhibit a relaxed working atmosphere. If you are going to use a fairly out-of-the-way place for a lengthy session remember to check on the availability of basic amenities and refreshments since even the most enthusiastic models can rapidly lose interest in a session if conditions are too spartan. If you find that either an outdoor or indoor location has potential but lacks, say, basic props, you can introduce items such as furniture to make it more suitable; the scope of an outdoor location, for instance, might be increased if you took along a wicker chair or a hammock perhaps, and an attractive but un-suitably furnished room could be made more effective by hiring or borrowing a nice chair or sofa or taking along flowers or pot plants.

An outdoor location possibly offers the greatest variety of backgrounds and settings, and natural surroundings can provide interesting contrasts of colour, texture and tone.

EXOTIC SETTINGS

*An exotic setting lends itself immediately to the creation of strong, rich images. In the shot of the sultry model by the waterfall (**below**) the gnarled tree-trunks, rough rock and white cascading water form an interesting textural background to the smooth skin of the girl. The lush vegetation, exotic fruits and primitive raft (**opposite**) combine to give rich tones and shapes.*

INDOOR DO'S AND DONT'S 1

There are two main differences in technique between outdoor and indoor photography: in indoor locations it is necessary to give more thought to how the subject will be lit and there is more restriction on the choice of camera angle and viewpoint. The simplest and most inexpensive method of lighting the nude indoors is by daylight from either a window or a skylight. This method of lighting is in fact particularly suitable for the nude as it can be used to create a soft and natural quality which effectively reveals the vital elements of form and texture, and studio lighting is often arranged to simulate the effect of daylight for this very reason.

The effectiveness and flexibility of daylight indoors will be greatly increased by the use of a few simple accessories. It will, for example, be very useful to have some means of diffusing the light from the window, especially if it is not north-facing and will be subjected to direct sunlight. This can be achieved by the use of a large sheet of tracing paper, frosted plastic or even a fine nylon mesh curtain. Another essential aid is at least one or two large white reflectors; these are in fact equally necessary for artificial lighting and can also be helpful when shooting outdoors. The reflectors can be simply large, white painted sheets of hardboard, masonite or rigid cardboard, but even more useful are the large 1-inch (2.5-centimetre) thick sheets of rigid foam polystyrene which are designed for insulation purposes and can be obtained from hardware stores. They are very light and can be propped against a chair, light stand or even a spare tripod. If one side of the reflector is painted matt black it can be used to screen excess light from the subject where a more contrasty effect is needed. As an alternative to this simple type of reflector there are the manufactured devices available from professional dealers in both matt white and with a silver finish for a stronger effect. The advantage of manufactured reflectors is that they are collapsible and portable and so can be used on location as well as indoors.

Another useful accessory is a mirror on an adjustable stand which can be positioned to create additional highlights as well as simply to fill in the shadows. As the only way of altering the direction of the light when shooting by window light is to alter the position of the camera and the model relative to the window, it is necessary to have a movable background. A painted or fabric-covered panel similar to the reflector would be adequate for head-and-shoulders shots but for full-length pictures it will be necessary to use the large rolls of background paper supplied by dealers; the paper can be draped in a smooth curve to avoid the sharp line which is created between wall and floor. The paper rolls are best supported on purpose-built units, available with tripod-type stands or spring-loaded poles which fit between floor and ceiling.

One of the problems associated with using daylight indoors is the substantial reduction in the brightness level compared to shooting outdoors. Although this can be overcome to a large extent by using faster film, a firm tripod is nevertheless a vital accessory. It will not only enable you to use slower shutter speeds without the fear of camera shake, but also to frame and focus the camera more precisely, while allowing you to give full attention to the model. As regards the type of head on the tripod, a pan and tilt head is a better choice than a ball and socket type as it is easier to adjust it accurately.

As regards camera equipment the requirements will not be very different from those for outdoor shots, although you will find long-focus lenses more restricted in use for all but head-and-shoulders shots. A wide-angle lens may be useful for shooting full-length shots in confined settings, but you will have to be careful about the way this is used: from a close viewpoint, for example, you can easily create

In a confined home studio
where space is usually at a
premium, the camera can be
positioned in an open doorway
and spring-loaded poles used
to support lights and reflectors
(**illustration, opposite left**).

INDOOR DO'S AND DONT'S 2

unpleasant perspective effects particularly if the camera is tilted up or down or if one part of the model's body is much closer to the camera than the rest of her. A zoom lens can be a useful accessory when you are shooting with the camera mounted on a tripod as it is much easier to use the zoom to adjust the framing of the image than to move the actual camera and tripod in relation to the model. For shooting in quite low light levels – daylight indoors, for instance – wide-aperture lenses will be an advantage, not only so that faster shutter speeds can be used but also to make focusing easier with a single lens reflex.

In addition to the things required for actually shooting the pictures it will be useful to have a few props and aids to posing: an easily portable sofa or bed, a stool or low-backed chair for head-and-shoulders pictures, and a low support such as a home-made plinth or even cushions which will extend the range of poses that the model can adopt. A few lengths of fabrics of varying colours and textures are also useful as they can be draped over supports and furniture to add variety. It is worth assembling a small collection of props to add both interest and colour – an attractive vase or pot that can be filled with flowers or a plant, and perhaps a small table that can be positioned in the background of the picture. You can get a good idea of the sort of objects that can be used effectively by simply looking through a few books and magazines that feature good nude photography to see how other photographers have used props to add interest and mood to their pictures.

A degree of artificial lighting can be introduced to supplement the daylight in order to control the contrast and effect, and even the existing room lighting such as a table lamp or a ceiling light can be used to reduce the density of the shadows cast by the daylight. Tungsten and daylight cannot be mixed when shooting in colour unless a blue filter is placed over the tungsten lights when shooting on daylight film; sheets of acetate colour correction filters can be obtained from dealers for this purpose. Fluorescent lighting, however, should be avoided for all but black-and-white shots as it will create a green cast on colour film. Although correction filters can be used to some effect this type of lighting is certainly not recommended as a suitable source for nude pictures. The colour quality of the daylight can also vary considerably, and with a north-facing window in particular there is a tendency for the higher colour temperature of such a light to create a blue cast on daylight film, resulting in rather cool skin tones. For this reason a colour correction filter such as an 81A or 81B is a useful accessory for daylight indoor photography as well as for outdoor pictures in certain circumstances.

A small flash-gun can also be used effectively as a fill-in light when shooting with daylight indoors with the advantage that its colour quality will mix quite satisfactorily with daylight. When using flash for this purpose it is important not to give full exposure to the flash as this will eliminate the shadows completely and create an artificial effect. The best procedure is to set the aperture at between one and two stops less than that indicated for the correct flash exposure and then use the shutter speed required to give the correct exposure for the lighter tones illuminated by the daylight. There is of course no reason why a small flash-gun cannot be used as the sole source of illumination for nude photography, either aimed directly at the model or reflected off a wall, ceiling or portable reflector. The first method will create little modelling if used close to the camera but if held above and to one side more defined shadows will be created within the subject. Direct flash is not usually the most pleasing lighting for normal use but it can create interesting effects and a quite pleasing quality if used in a considered way; David Bailey, for example, has used direct flash most effectively for some of his nude pictures. As a general rule, bounce or reflected flash will create a softer, more flattering light; a similar effect can be created by using a diffusing medium such as tracing paper or translucent white nylon between the flash-gun and the subject. A single light source is, however, relatively limiting in terms of the degree to which the quality and effect of the lighting can be controlled, and although a second or third small flash-gun can be added to increase the possibilities, the problem with such equipment is that it is not possible to see the effect that is being created, and this is very important when multiple sources are being used. For this purpose it is much more satisfactory to use studio-type lighting, either tungsten lights such as photofloods or halogen lamps or electronic flash with built-in modelling lamps; this will enable you to see the precise effect of your lighting arrangements and to make carefully controlled adjustments.

Indoor daylight can be supplemented to good effect with artificial lighting provided that acetate correction filters are used when shooting in colour.

OUTDOOR DO'S AND DONT'S 1

In many ways an outdoor location is the most satisfactory choice for a nude session since it frees you from many of the restrictions and concerns that indoor pictures impose. For example, there is much greater flexibility in terms of camera angles and viewpoints and it is not necessary to use lighting equipment, which also creates its own freedom. It is also much easier to find interesting backgrounds and settings to create more effective compositions without the effort and planning which are required for an indoor session. In many cases, too, the model will find an outdoor location more stimulating and easier to work in than the more sterile and restricted atmosphere of a studio. On the other hand, there are obvious disadvantages: first of all, you are at the mercy of the weather, and even if the light is good it may well be too cold for the model to work in comfort; secondly, it can be difficult to find a suitable place that is both easily accessible and reasonably private; and finally, it is important not to underestimate the problems involved for the model in managing and maintaining good hair and make-up throughout a lengthy session in the outdoors as well as looking after clothes and accessories and avoiding things getting creased and marked.

For all these reasons the key to a successful outdoor session is essentially a combination of good planning and reconnaissance, even if it is for only an hour or two. Since you will most likely be shooting somewhere far from your base, and also possibly from civilization, it is absolutely vital to have with you everything you will be likely to need, from equipment to film, props and clothes, and it is a good idea to write a comprehensive check list for both yourself and your model.

The choice of camera for an outdoor session will of course depend upon personal preference and the purpose of the photographs. While 35 mm is ideal for personal photography there are often circumstances in which for commercial reasons it is preferable to use the larger rollfilm formats. Cameras such as the Hasselblad have the additional advantage that they can be fitted with a Polaroid back which can be invaluable for checking the set-up before shooting on conventional film; this can be particularly important when a client or art director is present at the session as they will usually find it easier to assess the picture from a Polaroid than on the viewing screen. There are no particularly specialized requirements with regard to lenses for outdoor nude photography but as a general rule long-focus lenses will be found to be useful since they enable fussy and distracting details in the background areas to be controlled and subdued by differential focusing. As with indoor photography, a tripod is an invaluable aid to improving both the definition and the composition of pictures, and it is particularly important when long-focus lenses are used because the risk of camera shake is much greater. A separate hand meter is another useful accessory even if the camera has a built-in meter as it can be used to take close-up readings from the subject

without the need to move the camera and to take incident light readings in difficult situations. When you are away on a trip it is in any case reassuring to have a back-up metering system in case your equipment should fail.

A basic filter kit should be considered an essential part of the equipment for an outdoor session. The warm filters such as the 81A, B and C are especially valuable for controlling skin quality and should be used when shoot-

Good planning and careful preparation are vital to the success of an outdoor session, especially if the location is rather remote.

OUTDOOR DO'S AND DONT'S 2

ing on overcast days in open shade and against the light when the higher colour temperature of the daylight will tend to create a blue cast on colour film. Another useful type are the polarizing filters which can be very effective in creating richer and stronger blue skies. They are ideal for seaside locations when they can greatly improve the quality of water; used in combination with an 81B, for example, a polarizing filter can produce particularly rich skin tones and effects with tanned skin. When shooting in black-and-white an orange or red filter can be used in a similar way to create richer tones in blue sea and sky although they will tend to make skin and lips a paler tone. Both the soft focus attachment and the fog or pastel filter are useful devices when a softer, more romantic quality is required although soft focus effects can also be obtained by applying clear adhesive tape or petroleum jelly to the lens. Other attachments that might be effective on occasions but should not be over-used as they can appear gimmicky, are the star-burst and colour-burst filters which can create pleasing effects when the picture contains spectacular highlights such as the sparkle on back-lit water. The graduated filters are extremely valuable particularly for shots where the sky is important such as a sunset as they can be used to create richer and stronger tones and colours in the sky without affecting the foreground. A small selection of colour correction filters in a range of colours can also be useful for special effects.

In addition to basic camera equipment it is important to have some means of controlling the quality and contrast of the lighting and for this reason a portable reflector is a vital accessory. They are available in a variety of sizes and types, but remember that for full-length shots the reflector will need to be quite large to be effective, say 4 x 2 feet (1.2 x 0.6 metres). A large diffuser is also useful; this could quite simply be a piece of translucent white nylon stretched on to the same frame as the reflector and placed between the sun and the model. A small flash-gun can be used to fill in the shadows and in some circumstances can also be used to simulate the effect of sunlight on a dull day.

If you are planning to go away on a photographic trip, perhaps abroad, then the preparations and planning need to be even more thorough. It is vital to take two or perhaps three camera bodies and to ensure that you have sufficient stocks of spare batteries and film. Film requirements always tend to be greater than you anticipate and it is best to take more than you need since film bought from an unknown source abroad may have been badly stored or be from a substandard batch. To avoid any problems it is advisable to buy a batch of film from your regular dealer before you go and to test a roll to check the colour balance. Make sure that your camera equipment is covered for use abroad: some policies are for the home country only but can usually be extended for a specific period. It is also worth taking out holiday insurance for both yourself and the models since you may well be liable for any medical costs that they might incur while working for you.

It is sensible to assume that these responsibilities will fall to you, and you should remember to check passport validities, visas and vaccinations, and so on, since any mishaps in this direction are likely to affect you much more than the models. When travelling to a sunny location be particularly careful of the dangers of sunburn – most models like to sunbathe when they are not working and are not always as careful as they might be, and a sunburnt model is virtually useless.

Customs and security regulations can also be a problem when going on a trip. Some countries can be quite difficult if you try to take more than one camera, a couple of lenses and a few rolls of film through Customs, and the sight of a large silver case and a big bag of film can make officials react suspiciously. The safest method of avoiding harassment is to use an ATA Carnet. This is issued by the Chamber of Commerce in many countries and is in fact a temporary import licence. It is expensive, however, and an application for a licence takes some time to be processed. As a general rule it is adequate if you carry a full typewritten list in triplicate of all your equipment with serial numbers and descriptions which can be checked on entry and again on departure to ensure that nothing has been disposed of during your stay; in very difficult circumstances this list can be transferred into your passport if necessary. Airport security can also be a source of concern to the travelling photographer because of the widespread use of X-ray machines for checking hand baggage. In spite of the reassuring notices to the contrary these devices can and do fog unprocessed film, and although just one scan is unlikely to do any harm several doses will have a cumulative effect. As a sensible precaution it is best to pack your film in unbroken packs in a separate bag, get to the airport a little early and wait until the security checkpoint is not too busy and then simply ask very politely for this one item to be checked by hand. It is not advisable to allow your film to go into the luggage hold of the plane because these items are sometimes checked by a high-dosage X-ray machine that will without doubt fog the film.

Preparation and planning are the mainstays of a photographic trip. It is worth making a checklist of the equipment you will need to take with you, and ensuring that it is packed securely (**right**). Once on location, a Polaroid camera is extremely useful for recording ideas for pictures (**above**).

Packing equipment

An important part of preparing for a photographic trip is careful packing of cameras and equipment to prevent damage while you are travelling abroad. The best way of ensuring that equipment is protected but still remains accessible is to use two types of case: a rigid, shock proof case with compartment divisions for transporting equipment from one location to another; and a soft shoulder bag for use on the move.

Equipment checklist

Depending on the type of work to be done, a typical equipment checklist will contain some or all of the following pieces of equipment:

35 mm camera
Spare camera(s)
Variety of lenses, e.g. 400 mm, fast 55 mm, 180 mm, 16 mm fish-eye
Lens hoods, body and lens caps
Film in marked cans
Light meter
Filters, e.g. gelatin, graduated/neutral density
Portable flash
Flash sync cable
Spare batteries
Cable release
Motor drive extension cable
Blower brush
Tool kit

View camera
Variety of lenses, e.g. 90 mm wide-angle, 150 mm
Rail clamp
Double sheet film holders
Cable release
Polaroid back
Monorail
Lens holders
Gelatin filters
Bag bellows and standard bellows

THE
NUDE
INDOORS

THE BODY INDOORS

An indoor setting is arguably the most suitable for a nude session, especially for the amateur photographer, as privacy is guaranteed, which will produce a relaxed atmosphere for both photographer and model. The indoor setting can form an integral part of the picture, like a landscape in an outdoor shot. Indoor pictures can be lit in various ways: by daylight, portable studio lighting or a combination of both, and it can also be effective to use the ordinary room lighting.

HOME STUDIO 1

It is quite possible to take successful nude pictures in an ordinary indoor location but there are many situations in which a studio offers more control and flexibility, and the enthusiast will find some sort of studio facility a considerable advantage, either on a permanent basis or simply as a temporary makeshift arrangement. The first essential of a studio is to have clear space in which to arrange your lighting and backgrounds; remember that the height of a room can be just as important as its length and breadth. If you are going to have a temporary studio select a room from which the furniture can easily be cleared. It does not in fact have to be a room – a garage or even a large garden shed could well be used – and the actual amount of space required will be largely dependent on the type of pictures you want to take: head-and-shoulders shots or tightly framed body shots can be taken in a quite modest space, but full-length pictures will need considerably more. As an approximate guide, to shoot a full-length standing figure with a standard lens you will need to have at least 10 to 13 feet (3 to 4 metres) between the camera and the model, and in addition ideally at least another 6 feet (2 metres) between the model and the background. Do not forget that the camera can be positioned outside a doorway, for example, so that the room's actual dimensions could be slightly less. You will also find that a ceiling height of anything less than about 10 feet (3 metres) will be quite restricting when shooting a full-length figure especially when using lower than normal viewpoints. When considering the width of the room allow for the fact that the standard rolls of background paper are 9 feet (2.7 metres) wide and you will need a couple of yards each side of this in order to position the lights.

It will be necessary to eliminate the daylight when shooting with tungsten or electronic flash but the normal curtaining in a domestic room is usually sufficient. The floor can be a problem as if the room is carpeted you will find that when the model stands on the background paper it will crease and mark badly; a simple solution is to place a hardboard or masonite panel on top of the carpet before running the background paper down. The paper rolls can be supported on the specially designed units, either the tripod type or spring-loaded poles which fit between floor and ceiling. The advantage of the spring-loaded poles is that they take up less floor space, and for this reason they can also be useful as light stands. With a permanent studio facility it could be more convenient to have a wall-mounted background support bracket which takes up to three rolls, thus allowing rapid changing.

The choice of lighting equipment will largely be a question of personal preference and budget. The most inexpensive form of lighting, which is nevertheless versatile, are the simple floodlight reflectors on stands fitted with photoflood bulbs; these are similar to conventional domestic bulbs but are 'overrun' to give a much higher output in exchange for a much shorter working life of only a few hours. More efficient and powerful are the halogen lights which can be obtained in kit form consisting of two or three lights on folding stands with a variety of reflectors and attachments. An alternative is the studio electronic flash units which have built-in modelling lights; these are available either in the form of self-contained units such as the Bowens Monolight where each light has its own power pack, or the larger, more powerful equipment in which a single power pack fires a number of flash heads. The flash units can be triggered either by a synchronization lead or by an infra-red transmitter attached to the camera. When a number of flash units are used only one needs to be fired by the camera and the others can be simultaneously triggered by slave cells which fit into the sync sockets.

In addition to the lights themselves you will also need to consider the reflectors and attachments that can be used to control the quality of the light. In most circumstances in nude photography the light from a standard reflector will be found to be rather too hard for the main or key light and it will be necessary to have some means of diffusing it. The umbrella reflector is a popular means of achieving a softer light and can be fitted to most types of flash and tungsten halogen lights; the advantage of the umbrella reflector is that it provides a relatively large source of light but is easily portable. The window light or light box is another effective way of diffusing a light source; this is essentially a large square or rectangular reflector which fits over the light source and has a translucent plastic screen at the front. Where portability is not a consideration, however, it is relatively simple to construct a diffusion screen in the form of a large wooden frame about 6 x 3 feet (2 x 1 metres) covered in either tracing paper or frosted plastic. This can be propped against a light stand or tripod between the light source and the model and the degree of softness adjusted by altering the relative positions between them: a softer result will be achieved when the light is further from the screen. Although this type of diffusion screen is less convenient in use than the specially made attachments it can create a much softer light.

It is also essential to have one or two large reflectors in a home studio. These can either be the manufactured type or simply a large sheet of white painted card, hardboard, masonite or foam polystyrene. These can be used both to reflect light back into the shadow areas of the subject and to bounce the main light from it to create a soft diffused effect. As well as devices to make the light softer you will need reflectors that can create a harder or more confined light for rim-lighting and background effects, for example; honeycombs and snoots are useful in this respect, and for a really hard-edged light a spot light or spot attachment is ideal. In addition to the conventional light stands you will find it useful to have a boom arm stand which will enable you to position a light directly above the model's head for back-lighting or lighting the hair, and a low-level stand can also be useful for hiding a light behind the model to illuminate the background.

Space is the first requirement when setting up a home studio as there must be enough room to allow for flexible arrangement of the equipment and backgrounds.

HOME STUDIO 2

In most cases, it is possible to turn a domestic room into a studio without too much difficulty (**above**).

Expanding spring-loaded poles (**right**) can be used to support both background rolls and lighting. Tripod stands (**far right**) are available in a variety of sizes, heights and degrees of stability. A boom arm (**extreme right**) is the most common method of suspending lights over the subject.

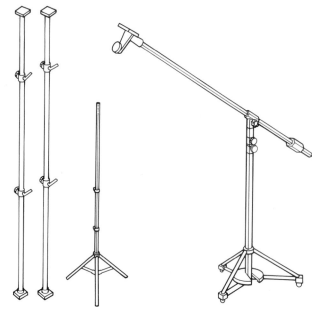

The ball and socket head (**above**) is an alternative to the pan and tilt mount (**top**), the most common type of tripod head.

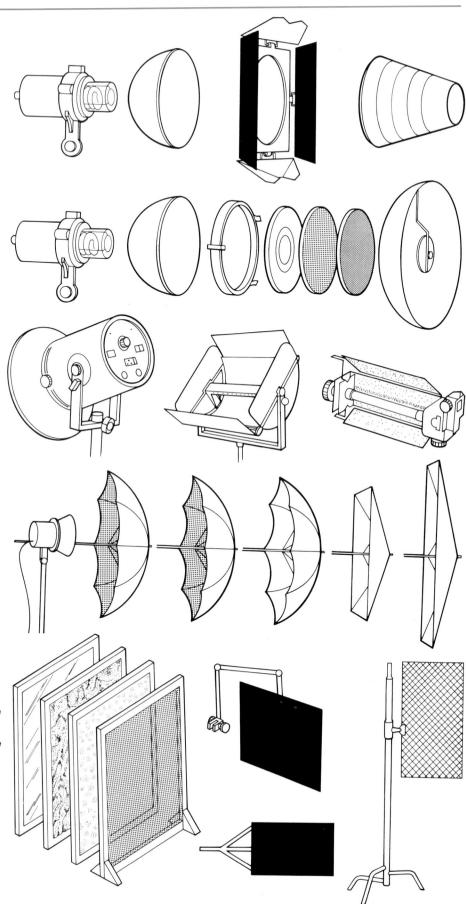

Electronic flash has largely superseded tungsten lighting in studio photography. The quality of the light can be modified by a variety of head attachments, to concentrate, diffuse or shape it. **Left to right)** *Flash tube with foil head; deep bowl reflector; barn doors; snoot.*

Left to right) *Flash tube; deep bowl reflector; opal diffuser; gauze diffuser; scrim; dished bowl with spiller cap.*

Left to right) *Bowens Monolight, a flash tube with integrated power pack and head; Lowell Softlight and Lowell Totalite, two tungsten lamps which provide the continuous lighting necessary in some circumstances.*

Umbrellas can be fitted in front of the light to provide broad, diffuse but unshaped lighting. **Left to right)** *Silvered umbrella; gold umbrella; translucent umbrella; square umbrellas.*

(Right) *A trace frame is a simple large-area diffuser covered with thin cloth or tracing paper.*

(Far right) *Shading devices can be suspended in front of a light to control the way it falls on to the subject. Various designs are available: French flag (**above**), gobo (**below**), yashmak (**extreme right**).*

PROFESSIONAL STUDIO 1

The only ways in which a professional studio is likely to differ from the studio facility which a keen amateur might have are in respect of the amount of space available, the convenience and the investment in equipment. As regards space, a great many professional photographers of the nude work in quite modestly sized studios; in fact, unless large sets or props are used there is often no real advantage in having a very large studio, as there is little that cannot be achieved in this field in a space of about 32 x 26 feet (10 x 8 metres). Convenience, on the other hand, is a vital consideration for the professional since both model time, studio time and the photographer's time are expensive commodities and anything that can reduce the amount of time wasted during a session is valuable. In terms of lighting, for instance, wheel-based stands would be more convenient than the tripod type, and some studios use the overhead tracking systems which keep the floor area free. A professional studio is likely to use the more powerful electronic flash packs; these not only have a greater output than the smaller units, which can be useful when using the larger formats since smaller apertures are often needed for adequate depth of field, but also have a very fast recycling time when used at the lower power settings which means that pictures can be taken in rapid succession. Most professional studios tend to favour electronic flash in preference to tungsten light, partly because the flash is so brief that the problem of camera shake and subject movement are virtually eliminated, and also because the flash generates less heat and the modelling lamps less glare than tungsten, making it more comfortable for the model.

As far as equipment is concerned, most studios will have a solid tripod or camera stand; the most common type is the wheel-based stand which enables the camera to be raised and lowered very quickly and easily. This has the added advantage that it can support the camera at up to 8 feet (2.5 metres) or more from the floor, facilitating high-viewpoint shots. In most professional studios there will be a wide selection of background paper rolls and wall flats which can be used to create instant sets, and many will have a stock of props and accessories for dressing a shot. As the model is a key element in this type of work there will usually be a model room where she can change and do her hair and make-up; this should be well lit and

A professional studio relies on convenience and usability in terms of both equipment and arrangement. Everything is chosen to minimize the amount of time wasted during a photographic session.

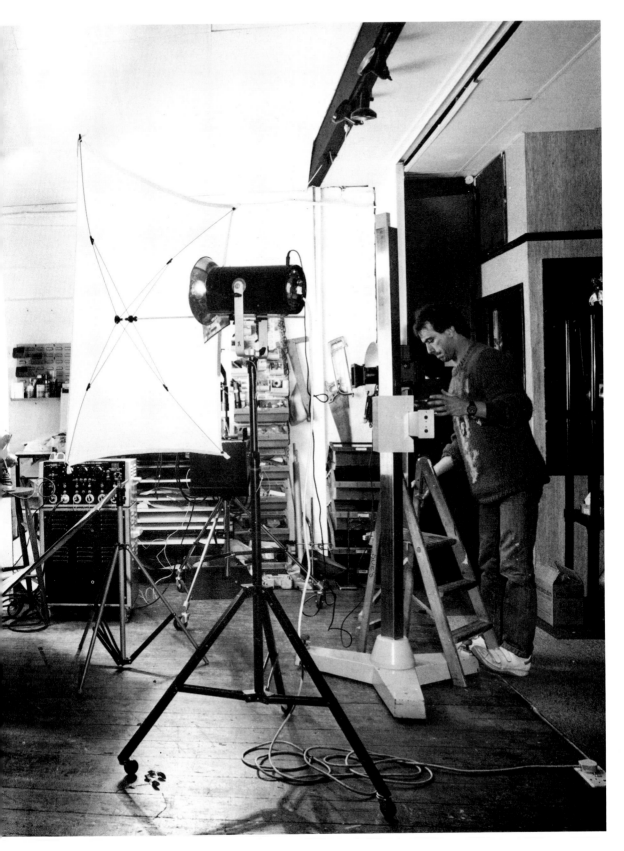

PROFESSIONAL STUDIO 2

have a full-length mirror and a garment rail or wardrobe to hang clothes and accessories. A selection of chairs, stools and other supports will also be found in most well-equipped studios, and in addition to conventional background papers many studios have a variety of fabrics and decorative or plastic laminates for use both as a background and as a surface on which the model can sit, kneel or lie; shiny black plastic laminate, for instance, can be very effective. A wind machine is a very useful accessory for nude work as it can be used to create a little life and movement in studio shots; these can be hired from specialist dealers but many photographers like to have one ready to hand. Another accessory which is perhaps used less often but is none the less useful for special effects is a front projection unit which enables a colour slide to be used as a background in studio shots. In terms of camera and lenses the professional will tend to have a wider variety of formats and also a greater number, as breakdowns are not unknown when equipment is used hard and frequently and a spare must always be to hand.

Although the 35 mm format is used in professional studios few photographers in this field would be limited to this size alone. The larger picture area of the roll film camera is often a considerable advantage, not only for the improvement in quality which it offers but also because both the photographer's clients and also the printer who reproduces the pictures can be prejudiced against 35 mm; it is, for example, easier to see the larger transparency without the need for projection and if any retouching or afterwork is needed this too will be much easier on the larger format than with 35 mm. It is important to appreciate that the professional's work will often be incorporated with lettering as part of a design, and often part of the background area must be left clear for this purpose; when the subject occupies only part of the frame it will be very small indeed with 35 mm. This is one reason why the square format camera such as the Hasselblad is so widely used as its shape enables the picture to be cropped in a variety of ways even to the extent of being able to decide later if a picture is to be a landscape or upright shape. A further advantage of the roll film SLR system is that most cameras of this type can be fitted with a Polaroid back to enable lighting set-ups and effects to be prejudged on a Polaroid before shooting on normal film.

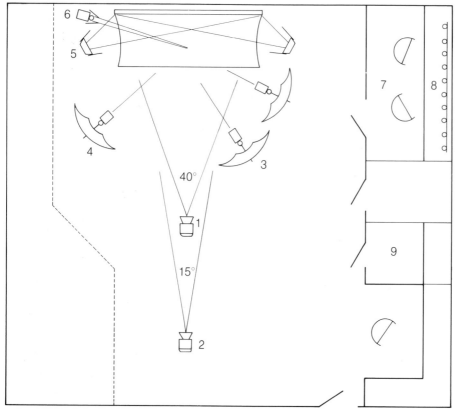

A floor plan is essential when designing the layout of a studio. The arrangement shown here (**left**) is for a portrait studio, in which the lighting requires a fair amount of space.

Portrait studio
1 Camera 1
2 Camera 2
3 Main light
4 Fill-in
5 Background striplight
6 Effects light
7 Dressing room
8 Dressing table and mirror
9 Film changing room

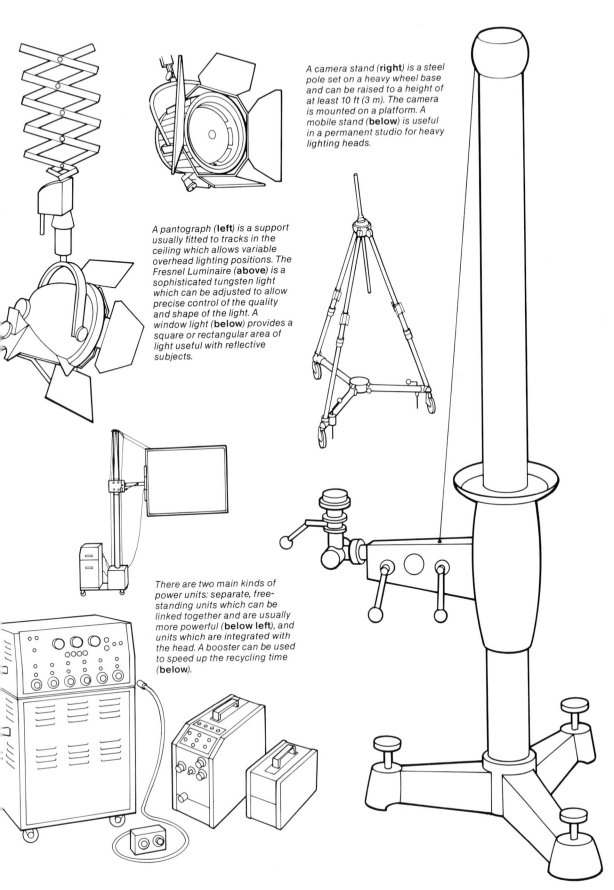

A camera stand (**right**) is a steel pole set on a heavy wheel base and can be raised to a height of at least 10 ft (3 m). The camera is mounted on a platform. A mobile stand (**below**) is useful in a permanent studio for heavy lighting heads.

A pantograph (**left**) is a support usually fitted to tracks in the ceiling which allows variable overhead lighting positions. The Fresnel Luminaire (**above**) is a sophisticated tungsten light which can be adjusted to allow precise control of the quality and shape of the light. A window light (**below**) provides a square or rectangular area of light useful with reflective subjects.

There are two main kinds of power units: separate, free-standing units which can be linked together and are usually more powerful (**below left**), and units which are integrated with the head. A booster can be used to speed up the recycling time (**below**).

CALENDAR SESSION

In recent years, many companies have started to use the glamour calendar as a tool to promote their products or services. The photographer who is commissioned to shoot the calendar has to meet exacting standards and he will experiment with many versions of a picture before both he and his client are satisfied. For this bedroom shot with its rich, romantic setting, the photographer took several different pictures of the model in the same pose before making the final choice.

OCTOBER

MON		5	12	19	26
TUE		6	13	20	27
WED		7	14	21	28
THU	1	8	15	22	29
FRI	2	9	16	23	30
SAT	3	10	17	24	31
SUN	4	11	18	25	

NOVEMBER

MON	30	2	9	16	23
TUE		3	10	17	24
WED		4	11	18	25
THU		5	12	19	26
FRI		6	13	20	27
SAT		7	14	21	28
SUN	1	8	15	22	29

DECEMBER

MON		7	14	21	28
TUE	1	8	15	22	29
WED	2	9	16	23	30
THU	3	10	17	24	31
FRI	4	11	18	25	
SAT	5	12	19	26	
SUN	6	13	20	27	

What a fantastic night out . . . he seems really interested in me . . . thinks I could go a long way . . . films seen . . . heard that before. Hope his client likes the pictures . . . and he did let me keep the knickers . . . lunch tomorrow with him, yes . . . oh well sweet dreams . . .

BASIC TO EXOTIC 1

Any interior, however basic,
lends itself to successful nude
photographs. These three
pictures illustrate the different
visual effects obtained from
three contrasting settings: the
most basic, where the
combination of dramatic
lighting against a plain
background has produced a
strong image (**left**); the interior
of a derelict villa, with the rough
walls forming a textural
contrast to the model's skin
(**right**); and a softly lit, old-
fashioned interior which
conveys a gentle, introspective
mood (**below**).

BASIC TO EXOTIC 2

Three more elaborate interiors
have produced a different
effect in the final image. The
Victorian bedroom with its
ornate wall and bed coverings
has a rich, romantic quality
(**below**), while the luxurious
decor of the two other pictures
with the heavy drapes and
stylized furniture has created a
more glamorous, overtly erotic
atmosphere.

CREATIVE CHOICE

You only need to look through books and magazines
which feature nude photography to see how important the
choice of setting is to both the mood and effect of a
picture. In some cases the setting can almost dominate
the style of a photograph – the slick, sophisticated interiors
of Helmut Newton contrasted with the folky, rural settings
of David Hamilton, for example – where the setting appears
to dictate not only the atmosphere and quality of the
photograph but also the choice and personality of the
model. For this reason it is worth taking the time and
trouble to consider the potential of various rooms and
settings in a fairly analytical way. The average family house
consists of living-room, bedrooms, kitchen, bathroom, hall
and stairs and a dining-room, and in certain circumstances all of these rooms can make a useful contribution
to a picture as they are usually furnished and decorated in
quite different ways.

*The choice of a setting plays an
important role in the creative
effect of a picture. A setting with
a defined character, such as the
Victorian drawing-room (**right**),
can dictate the atmosphere of
the photograph. It also
influences the style and
approach of the model, as in the
two cottage interiors (**above**)
where the simplicity of the
setting has produced a natural,
relaxed pose.*

BEDROOMS

A bedroom forms an obvious setting for nude photography, especially if the sexual aspect of the image is to be emphasized, and also because the furnishings and decorations will usually be pleasingly soft and evocative. The bed itself is often an ideal setting, not only for the immediate sexual and even erotic connotations but also because it provides the model with a situation in which she can be completely flexible and unrestricted in the way she poses and moves her body. A large mirror can also add both interest and impact to a bedroom shot; as well as simply making use of the reflected image, a decorative mirror such as a cheval glass could be used as a key prop in a picture, forming the main element of the composition.

The different styles of bedroom have created markedly contrasting pictures. The rich, luxurious furnishings have a glamorous, almost decadent effect (below), whereas the ornate Victorian setting produces a more romantic mood, with the mirror being used to add an effective voyeuristic element (opposite).

BATHROOMS 1

The bathroom is almost a natural place for taking nude pictures if only for the reason that it is of course ideal for wet shots; it provides a logical setting and also means that the model can get very wet without the problems this would obviously cause in any other room. Showers and baths are therefore understandably popular settings for nude pictures and the textural and photographic qualities of wet skin are considerable. The problem in most bathrooms, however, is that both lighting and camera angles are usually very restricted because of the limited space unless you are lucky enough to own or have access to a really large bathroom. Often the most practical way of dealing with the lighting is to use bounce flash from a wall or ceiling although that can give a rather excessively soft, bland light unless care is taken, particularly in a room with light, reflective decor. The problem of camera angles can sometimes be solved by removing the door or by using a mirror to create a longer throw. When shooting in bathrooms you must also be particularly careful to avoid unwanted reflections in shiny surfaces and mirrors as these can be very distracting.

A mirror can be used to good effect in a bathroom shot to overcome the problem of restricted camera angles.

BATHROOMS 2

A bathroom or shower offers a surprising number of photographic possibilities, as these pictures show. The setting of cool marble, mosaic and gilt fitments has produced a sophisticated image (**left**), while isolating the model in front of the mirror as she applies her make-up has created a more intimate and personal picture (**above**). In the shower shot (**right**) the skilful use of lighting has emphasized the lines of the model's body.

OTHER ROOMS 1

Even a kitchen need not be considered entirely inappropriate for nude photography, especially if a light-hearted or even abstract approach is adopted. The glossy, highly sophisticated quality of a modern kitchen, for example, can be exploited quite effectively in the right type of picture, with reflective steel or laminated surfaces being used as backgrounds or as part of the composition, while in total contrast the warm, homely atmosphere of a farmhouse-style kitchen, perhaps furnished in pine, could create a quite different mood.

The living-room is one of the more obvious interior settings not only because a nude will probably look more natural and less unexpected than in the kitchen but also because the room is usually larger and more convenient to shoot in and the decor and furnishings will create a more relaxed and sympathetic environment. Curtains and drapes, for example, will often provide an effective background or prop in a picture, and so will a nice sofa or easy chair; a luxurious carpet or rug can also be used to good effect, and if the room has an open fireplace that could create both atmosphere and interest.

The hall and stairway can be useful if only for the reason that they usually have less conventional proportions than an ordinary room and reveal interesting shapes and corners, as well as the opportunity of using different levels both to position the model and to enable high and low camera angles. A particularly decorative stairway offers many possibilities and can make a much more dominant contribution to the composition and mood of a picture.

The possibilities afforded by a dining-room are essentially similar to those of a living-room except that the more functional and formal furniture is likely to be more restricting, though this too can be used effectively in some situations, particularly if it has rich grain and texture such as antique mahogany.

*The busy detail of this farmhouse kitchen, with the warm tones of the pine woodwork and contrasting colours of the pastel flowers and blue china, has created an inviting, homely atmosphere (**opposite**). Even a hallway can provide a setting; here the highly polished tiled floor has formed an effective background to the model (**right**).*

OTHER ROOMS 2

A living-room can provide a series of ready-made settings as it usually offers both sufficient space and enough furniture and angles for interesting backgrounds. An open fireplace or a mirror, for example, can be used as the focal point in the image.

PATIOS AND BALCONIES

It is worth bearing in mind that the settings and backgrounds of a shot do not necessarily have to be sensible or logical and they can also be used for deliberately contrived and dramatic effects where unexpected juxtapositions can create a bold or bizarre quality. If handled with a little panache, quite unrelated objects can be used as props or combined to produce semi-abstract or ambiguous pictures which can tease the viewer's imagination. When considering the potential of a room do not forget to take into account the possibilities afforded by the windows; these can contribute to the composition and mood of a picture as well as to the lighting, particularly if you have French windows, for instance, or recessed garret-style or casement windows. Sometimes these types of windows are accompanied by a small balcony or patio and these too can provide an effective setting. Curtains and blinds can also be included, both to form backgrounds and to create lighting effects, for example the bars of light formed by the slits in a venetian blind or the textured effect of light and shade produced by a coarse mesh curtain.

In addition to using rooms in the conventional sense you might also consider the possibilities of perhaps a garden shed, garage, boxroom or an attractive conservatory for atmospheric pictures. An empty room that has been cleared of furniture for decorating can also be put to effective use, and old derelict houses have often provided successful settings for nude pictures, as elements like broken windows, peeling plaster, cracked woodwork and bare floorboards can be surprisingly evocative for certain types of photograph.

A venetian blind can create interesting visual effects in an image. Here the stripes of the blind are echoed in the model's glasses.

The marble wall and tile floor in the corner of this patio provide an effective background to this portrait shot.

In this shot, the intricate ironwork of the ornamental balcony forms an interesting textural contrast to the lace of the model's wrap.

BOLD EFFECTS 1

As a genre, nude photography is particularly suitable for photographers who like to shock or surprise with their pictures. Even in these enlightened times an element of naughtiness still attaches to the nude and when it is used with other elements which create bold or unexpected effects the result can be very powerful indeed. There are a number of ways of achieving this in a picture – deliberately erotic images, for example, will always attract attention and invite comment. This does not necessarily mean, however, that such pictures have to be explicit, in fact in this context implication can be more effective since sexual response is very largely a product of the imagination and a picture which stimulates the imagination is likely to be more erotic than one that simply records visual information. Photography also has an advantage over other graphic media in that it can very effectively convey the impression of texture in an image. In this way a photograph can be used to provoke a tactile response from the viewer as well as a purely visual one. Lighting which emphasizes the texture of a model's skin, for example, will invariably create a degree of impact in a picture. Texture can also be enhanced by juxtaposition with other textures, skin and silk together in a picture, for instance, while the same applies to many popular images like wet or oiled skin, fur and leather and so on; indeed, fetishism is a very powerful erotic element and is often associated with textures.

Another way of creating bold effects in a picture is by exploiting the element of surprise, using a model in a strange or unexpected setting or juxtaposing her with other objects. This approach to nude photography is limited only by the photographer's imagination and taste and his ability to make it work. It is very hard to draw the line between a powerful and meaningful picture and one that is merely silly or banal, and the decision is also very subjective. It is not difficult to think of potentially startling situations like a nude girl tied to a cross for instance, as photographed by John Swannell, but it is quite another thing to shoot pictures of this type with taste and conviction and to make other people see them in the same light.

*There are many ways of introducing bold effects into a nude picture. One obvious way is by the choice of a deliberately provocative pose for the model, enhanced by her accessories (**above right**). Another technique is by the juxtaposition of fabrics such as silk or fur against the skin (**right**), or strange or unexpected props can be used to create an element of shock (**opposite**).*

BOLD EFFECTS 2

The arresting effect of this
double exposure of a nude and
a seascape (**right**) was made in
a slide duplicator. By contrast,
careful framing and the model's
suggestive pose have created a
strongly erotic effect in the
abstract nude shot (**below**).

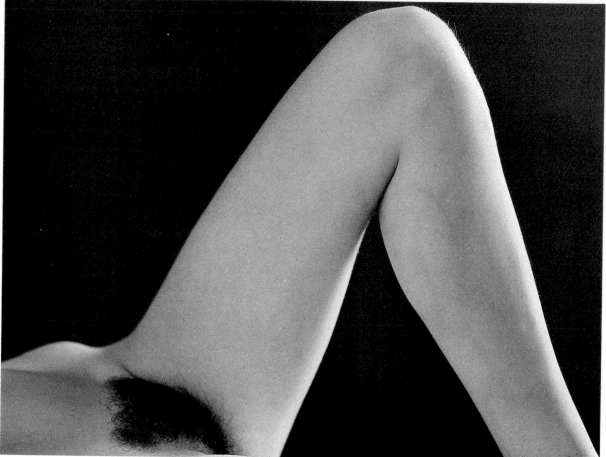

This startling, even disturbing image relies on the shock effect of the model's pose and accessories (**above**), while the impact of the nude figure under the shower results from the choice of lighting which emphasizes the texture of the model's wet skin (**left**).

LIGHTS AND LIGHTING

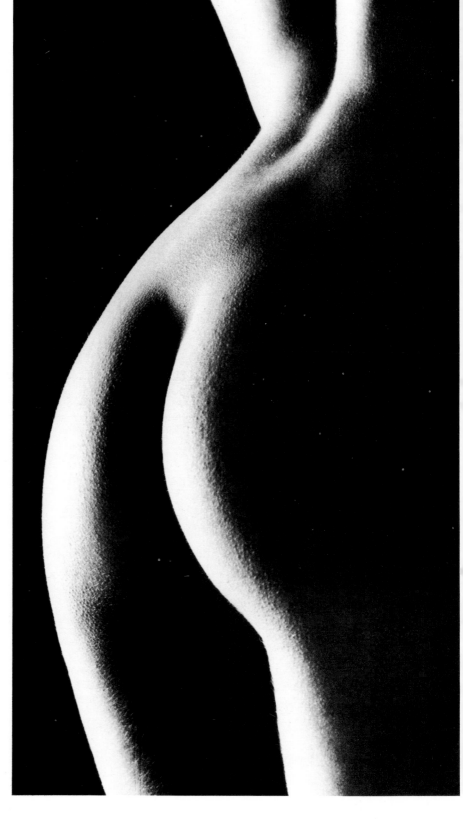

The direct light of an undiffused light positioned behind the model is used in this abstract nude shot (**right**); the black background emphasizes the outline of the model's body. The nude torso (**opposite above**) was lit by one light positioned slightly behind and to the left of the model behind a large tracing-paper screen. In the head-and-shoulders portrait (**opposite below**) an un-diffused tungsten light, fitted with a snoot, was positioned slightly to the right of the camera and just above the model's eye level to emphasize her cheek-bones. A second light, to the right and behind the model, fitted with a snoot, has created the highlights on her hair.

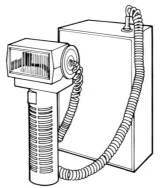

(**Top**) *Manual flash units (**left**) have a fixed output, while automatic units (**right**) have a sensor which measures the light reflected from the subject, controlling the duration of the flash for automatic exposure adjustment.*

(**Left**) *A wet cell unit has a large, rechargeable battery which is carried on a shoulder strap. It gives greater power and rapid recharging between flashes.*

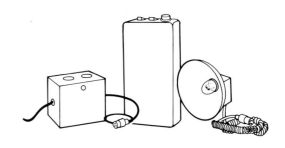

Guide no.80		Guide no.160
f4	20ft (6m)	f8
f8	10ft (3m)	f16
f16	5ft (1.5m)	f32

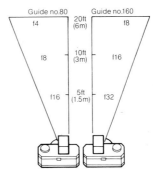

(**Above**) *The recycling battery unit has a very high output and recharges rapidly.*

(**Left**) *Guide numbers provide a method of calculating flash exposures. Most flash units have a guide number indicated in feet or metres which relates to a specific film speed. To calculate the exposure, divide the guide number by the distance between the flash and the subject.*

USING FLASH

Flash can be used to create a variety of effects in an indoor location. A single flash bounced from the ceiling reduces the unflattering shadows caused by harsh, directional light (**below**). A diffused flash close to the camera is balanced by a second flash behind the model aimed at the background (**bottom**). In the indoor shot (**right**), daylight is balanced will fill-in flash. For the studio shot (**opposite**), one flash is aimed at the white background and a diffused flash from 45° to the camera angle, with a white reflector on the other side to fill in the shadows.

COLOUR IN ACCESSORIES

An obvious way of introducing a vigorous quality into a nude photograph is by using brightly coloured accessories. These can make a strong impact in an image when contrasted against skin tones.

LENS EFFECTS

Flare is an effect that is usually considered to be a fault. It is caused when a bright light falls directly on to the front of the lens causing light to be scattered indiscriminately within the lens producing a lowering of contrast and colour saturation and often accompanied by streaks of light from the source. It is commonly experienced, for example, when shooting into the sun, particularly when the sun is close to the edge of the picture or within it. However, if flare is used in a considered and controlled way it can produce a quite pleasing effect and it can be judged fairly accurately when using an SLR, for example.

The use of lenses of different focal lengths can also introduce an unusual or dramatic quality into a picture, largely because it enables you to control the effect of perspective. Pictures taken with a standard lens present a view of the subject which is close to that which we experience visually in that we perceive an impression of depth and distance by the fact that objects of a similar size appear to become smaller the further they are from the camera. This effect is heightened when we approach the foreground objects more closely and diminished when we are further away from them; with the model close to the camera, for instance, a distant tree would appear to be much smaller than the model and as the camera is moved further away it would become progressively larger than the model. With a wide-angle lens, for example, the subject can be approached very closely and more distant details

still be included. This has the effect of greatly exaggerating the effect of perspective to the extent that some parts of the model's body or even her face can be made to appear disproportionately larger than others; Bill Brandt's famous distorted nudes were done in this way. Even more bizarre effects can be achieved with ultra-wide-angle lenses or fish-eye lenses. The opposite effect is achieved with long telephoto lenses as they enable a distant viewpoint to be used and close foreground details to be excluded, and the result can be almost to eliminate the effect of perspective and the impression of depth, creating pictures in which there can appear to be a compression of planes.

There are also a wide variety of lens attachments which can create different effects; these can be obtained individually or as part of a filter system such as the Cokin. Devices like the star-burst filter can be used to add interest to a picture by creating star-shaped streaks of lights from highlights, while the colour-burst or diffraction grating creates a similar effect with rainbow-coloured streaks of light. Other useful attachments include multiprisms which create a number of repeated images of the subject in different configurations, and special colour filters with clear spots in the centre which allow the subject or the central part of the image to be recorded normally but with the rest of the picture given a colour cast. However, all of these devices should be used with discretion as otherwise they can appear somewhat gimmicky.

The different types of lenses can be manipulated to introduce many different qualities into an image. These three examples were taken with a 35 mm wide-angle lens (**left**); a standard lens with cross-lighting (**right**); a standard lens with the model standing on a mirror to create the distortion (**above**).

SOFT FOCUS EFFECTS

Soft focus is probably one of the most simple and widely used effects in the field of nude photography. As well as creating a pleasing quality in its own right it also has the particular advantage of masking any slight flaws in the model's skin and of being a quite flattering effect generally. There are a wide variety of attachments which can be bought as part of a filter system such as the Cokin, or separately such as the Zeiss Softar. The basic principle, however, is the same: a piece of clear glass or plastic engraved or moulded with an interference pattern is placed over the camera lens and creates a degree of diffusion. The effect is quite different from that of an out-of-focus image as there is an underlying core of sharpness which is surrounded by a softer effect. As a result the image appears quite clear but fine detail is subdued; in addition it can cause highlight areas to 'bleed' slightly into the darker tones which can create a pleasing halo-like effect when shooting into the sun or when the subject is back-lit. Another by-product of the soft focus attachment is that it tends to reduce both contrast and colour saturation, producing images with a more mellow quality; this can be particularly helpful when a more harmonious colour quality or romantic mood is required.

In addition to manufactured attachments there are a number of other widely used methods of producing soft focus effects and professional photographers often prefer these. Clear adhesive tape can be stretched across the front of the lens mount or across the lens hood with a small clear area left in the centre to allow a degree of sharpness to be retained. Another method is to smear clear petroleum jelly on to a filter or piece of thin glass placed over the lens, again with a clear area left in the centre; the advantage of this method is that the jelly can be swirled around with a finger-tip to vary the effect, which in addition to producing soft focus can also create interesting streaks from highlights in the image. Other widely used materials are nylon mesh (as used in ladies' tights, for example) and plastic film or thin plastic sheeting. The fog or pastel filter also creates a similar effect to the soft focus attachment; it has little or no effect on the definition of the image but will reduce the contrast and colour saturation quite considerably.

Soft effects can also be introduced into the image by using blur, either in the background or surrounding details or in some cases within the main subject. This can be achieved in a number of ways. Shallow depth of field is perhaps the most basic. By using a wide aperture and preferably a long-focus lens and focusing on the model it is possible to throw other details that are closer to or further from the camera well out of focus, and this can produce quite exciting effects, for example when the foreground and background contain brightly coloured or contrasting details such as shooting through a foreground of flowers. Another method is to use slow shutter speeds, which will allow parts of the subject that are moving to be recorded as a blur but with the static elements quite sharp.

With a model running across the camera you can, for instance, pan the camera so that she is recorded quite sharply while the background or surroundings are blurred. Alternatively, you could have the model static against a moving background such as a waterfall and with the camera mounted on a tripod use a slow shutter speed to create a blurred background. When using a zoom lens you can also create an unusual blurred effect by moving the zoom setting of the lens from the shortest to the longest focal length during the exposure; as this is likely to need a fairly slow shutter speed it is usually easiest to shoot with the camera mounted on a tripod. Another interesting variation on the blur effect is to combine flash with daylight, using a slow shutter speed and a moving subject. In this way where the light from the flash predominates there will be a sharp image and where the daylight predominates the image will be blurred. The exact effect of this technique is a little unpredictable and it is wise to vary both the speed of the movement and also the shutter speed settings.

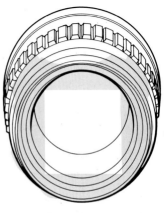

There are a number of ways of creating soft focus effects in an image, all of which produce a pleasing quality. One of the manufactured attachments can be used (**top**), but it is also possible to achieve the same effect (**opposite**) by means of a home-made method such as stretching clear adhesive tape across the front of the lens, as shown in the illustration above. In the studio shot of the dark-skinned model against a white background (**left**) a soft salmon-pink filter was used on the catchlight, with the key light directed from the right.

USING FILTERS

As well as using colour correction filters to offset a potential colour cast it is also sometimes effective to use filters to introduce a deliberate colour bias, and in some instances this can be used to contribute to the mood of a picture. For this purpose the gelatin filters which are available in both the primary and complementary colours in a wide range of strengths are very convenient since they can introduce either a very subtle or a pronounced colour cast. In some circumstances it can be effective to achieve this colour cast by shooting on the wrong type of film for the light source – shooting on tungsten-balanced film in daylight, for example, will produce a strong blue cast, and daylight type film in artificial light will create a strong orange cast. For even more bizarre results infra-red film, available in both colour and black-and-white emulsions, can be used to good effect. When used with the recommended Wratten 12 filter (a strong yellow) the colour version will produce quite strange colour effects: skin tones, for example, will appear fairly normal but green foliage will record as a magenta tone. The effect can be varied by using other filters and it will also vary according to the lighting conditions and the exposure level. The black-and-white version of the film can also produce interesting effects – used with a red filter it will record blue skies as almost black and green foliage as white – and it is particularly effective when used with subjects that have a landscape element. The film is also quite grainy and this can be used to add further impact and interest to a shot.

In fact grain alone can be very effective in some circumstances, in both colour and black-and-white pictures. The technique is simple enough: use a fast film, possibly push-processing it to increase both its speed and the grain size, and compose your picture so that only a small proportion of the film is used. This means that it can be enlarged considerably which will of course increase the effect of the grain; one way of doing this is to frame the picture using a long-focus lens and then to switch to a wide-angle for the actual exposure.

Another interesting way of altering the colour quality of a picture is to use filtered flash when shooting in daylight. The technique is similar to that of fill-in flash except that where the flash exposure is used to illuminate the foreground (the model) and the daylight exposure records the background details, a colour filter is placed over the camera lens to create a colour cast – say a blue filter – and a filter of the opposite hue (in this case, yellow) is placed over the flash-gun; the colour cast will be eliminated in those parts of the image which are illuminated by the flash, i.e. the foreground model, leaving the more distant areas with the blue colour cast.

As well as utilizing the infra-red wavelengths of light to create colour effects it is also possible to make use of the ultra-violet band of the spectrum to create interesting images. An ultra-violet light source is needed for this technique, of the type that emits 'black light' which is often used in window displays and discos, for example. The

technique works on the principle that ultra-violet light 'excites' fluorescent material and causes it to 'glow'. As this lighting effect is of a much lower intensity than normal light levels this type of shot has to be set up in a darkened room and the UV lamp will have to be placed quite close to the model. Even with a fast film such as Ektachrome 200 you will find that quite slow shutter speeds are needed, so a tripod will also be necessary. It is best to use daylight type film and also a UV absorbing filter to eliminate scattered UV light as you only want to record the fluorescence. The fluorescent materials can be introduced either as props – fluorescent dyes are used in many fabrics, for instance – or objects can be painted with fluorescent colours which are available from art stores. The model could also use these colours on herself as make-up, on the fingernails, for example, or in her hair.

Filtration can be used to create a variety of interesting effects in an image, such as a spectral star nebula filter which splits the spectrum (above), a starburst filter (right), and an ultra-violet filter used in combination with an ultra-violet light source and fluorescent materials (opposite).

BLACK-AND-WHITE 1

Most experienced photographers would agree that it is quite difficult to shoot both black-and-white and colour pictures during the same session, for the simple reason that each requires a quite different approach, and switching from one to the other on alternative rolls of film involves both effort and concentration. The quality of a good black-and-white print lends itself admirably to the applications of nude photography although its value lies perhaps more in the realm of personal expression than a commercial context. One reason why the nude and black-and-white materials combine so successfully is that the elements of line, shape, form and texture, which can be exploited to the full in a nude photograph, are particularly effective in the black-and-white medium, and in this context the presence of colour in the image can detract from the basic elements. What is more, the black-and-white medium is particularly flexible in the ways that the tonal quality of the image can be controlled and manipulated. Another consideration that may be overlooked is that colour photographs have become extremely commonplace. It is a relatively simple matter for even an inexperienced photographer to expose a roll of colour negative film, send it to a laboratory for processing and get back a batch of good-quality colour prints. The black-and-white process, on the other hand, is in many ways both more difficult and more rewarding where high-quality results are concerned and as most people are in general less familiar with the medium it is an ideal vehicle for more personally motivated and interpretative work.

*The black-and-white medium lends itself well to the creation of effective nude photographs. Three effects are shown here: in the first example, the model was lit against a bamboo background (**top**); the low-key effect of the second picture (**right**) relies largely on the dark tones of the image in the dark skin of the model and the dark-toned background paper; while the use of a stark white background and even frontal lighting has provided the ideal contrast to the model's fish-net tights (**opposite**).*

BLACK-AND-WHITE 2

The elements of line, form and texture are shown to particular effect in these three pictures. the back-lit silhouette shot against a white background (**opposite**) emphasizes the smooth lines of the model's body; the illustration (**left**) shows two typical lighting set-ups for creating a silhouette. In the abstract female nude shot (**below left**), a light positioned to the right of the model has allowed the shadows to go dark, creating interesting shapes and accentuating the skin texture. In the shot of the male torso (**below right**), the key light is placed at an acute angle to the right of the model, with a reflector on the left.

MULTIPLE IMAGES

Where a more abstract type of picture is required it can be achieved effectively in many instances by combining two or more images. This can be done in a number of ways, perhaps the easiest being simply to make two or more exposures on to the same piece of film. Ideally this requires a camera which enables the double exposure prevention mechanism to be bypassed, although it is possible to wind the film back and run it through the camera again after the first exposure; this is rather tricky, however, and the starting position of the film must be marked accurately in the first place. The success of this technique depends largely on the way the images are juxtaposed, and it is best to use a camera with a viewing screen so that the position of the first image can be traced on to it with a marking pen to make it easier to line up the second image. As a general rule the technique is most effective either when the light tones of one image are juxtaposed against the darker tones of the other, or when one image is used as a more subdued background detail and the other is allowed to dominate – for example, a quite well-lit nude torso could be double exposed effectively on to a dark-toned wood grain to create a textured effect. It is also important to appreciate that as each additional exposure will have a cumulative effect they should be decreased to avoid the final image being over-exposed; reducing one exposure more than the other will also help to make the lighter image more dominant than the darker image. Another way of using this technique in the studio is to place the model against a black background in a darkened room and to make two or more exposures, allowing her to move between each exposure. This can be used to create a stroboscopic effect and it is not necessary to reduce individual exposures since the black background means that each image is effectively being photographed on to unexposed film.

A projector can also be used in a number of ways to create a multiple image. This technique has to be carried out in a darkened room and artificial light type colour film used with a tungsten projector. One method which can be particularly effective with the nude is to project an image on to her body and simply rephotograph the result. If the model is placed against a black background the projected image will show the model's outline quite clearly, but if she is placed against a white background the projected image will continue over the background creating a more subtle effect. The position of the projector will also have an effect on the nature of the image: if it is placed close to the camera it will create a quite flat result with little indication of modelling within the model's body, but if it is positioned at an angle to the camera a more three-dimensional effect will be created. It is also possible to introduce more interest into the image by using some studio lighting to illuminate parts of the body. In this way the projected image will appear to blend with the image of the model since the projected image will be erased where the lighting predominates. This lighting needs to be controlled quite tightly so that it illuminates only small selected areas of the subject and is not allowed to be scattered indiscriminately which would degrade the projected image. For this reason it is best to fit the lights either with a snoot or cardboard cones or to use a spotlight; rim-lighting or back-lighting is particularly effective for this effect.

Another way of using a projector is to project a slide of the model on to another surface and rephotograph this; this can create a textured or distorted effect or the nude can be made to appear as part of an object. For example, the slide could be projected on to a piece of crumpled paper to create a distorted image or on to a light-toned object in a still-life arrangement. A projector can also be used to create a more realistic background effect in which a slide of an outside location can form part of the image in a studio shot of a model. There are essentially two ways of doing this. The first is to place a large translucent screen behind the model and the projector behind this, with the selected slide sized and focused on to the screen. The model is then lit in the normal way but taking great care that the lighting does not spill on to the screen as this will degrade the projected image; for this reason it is also necessary to ensure that there is some distance between the screen and the model. A more satisfactory method is to use front projection. This requires the use of a device with a semi-silvered mirror which fits on to the front of the camera. The projector is placed at right angles to the camera and with the aid of the mirror projects the background transparency along the optical path of the camera. This is then focused on to a highly reflective screen which is placed behind the model who is lit in the normal way, again ensuring that light does not spill on to the screen. A specially manufactured version of this equipment with a projector illuminated with electronic flash is used in many professional studios to create outdoor backgrounds as well as many more abstract effects.

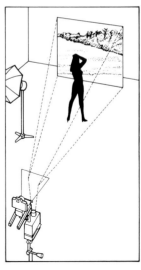

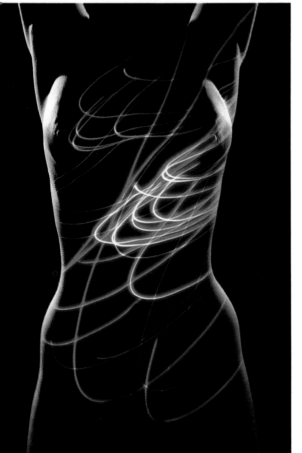

There are various methods of creating a multiple image: multiple exposures made one after the other on to the same piece of film (**opposite**); a slide sandwich (**top**); a physiogram (**far left**); using a mirror in front of the camera lens to create a double image (**left**); projecting a slide on to the subject to produce a textured effect (**below**). Front projection is a method of using a colour transparency as the background of a studio shot; the illustration (**above**) shows the typical set-up.

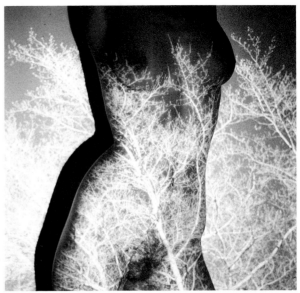

THE
NUDE
OUTDOORS

CHOOSING A LOCATION 1

Choosing a suitable setting for a nude session is a vital factor upon which the ultimate success of the pictures can depend, and it therefore warrants careful consideration. With the concern for both privacy and access uppermost in your mind you must from the outset have a clear idea of the type of pictures you want to take in order to be able to weigh up the potential of various locations and to see them in terms of actual pictures rather than simply as a scene. The essential nature of the place you choose will have an influential effect on both the type of pictures you take and the mood and effect they create, regardless of the choice of model or any photographic techniques that you might apply; a session in a woodland setting, for example, would have a quite different outcome from a session on a beach. It may appear an obvious point but it is worth bearing in mind that the basic colour quality of the pictures can often be determined by the nature of the setting – for example, it would be difficult to avoid a predominance of green in a woodland setting just as it would blue in a Mediterranean beach location. You will obviously be able to introduce other colours but the overall tone of the session is likely to be set by the initial choice of location.

Unless you are setting out to produce a particular image for a specific purpose then it is also important to consider the ways in which a location or setting can be used to create variety, particularly when an all-day session is planned. In a beach location, for example, do not just look for a nice expanse of sand but see if there are other features that you will be able to use such as a fishing boat or an outcrop of rocks. In this way you will be able to take a series of shots all within a distance of a few yards but each looking as if it were taken in a completely different setting. The lighting is another important consideration: in bright sunlight, for instance, you may find that certain viewpoints and camera angles are only possible at a certain time of day and this can be a problem when setting up a specific shot, for example shooting with a sunset over the sea as a background would be futile on an east-facing beach. You should also bear in mind when choosing a location that it might appear less attractive if the lighting conditions on the day of the shoot are different from when you first saw it. A beach seen on a bright, sunny day under a blue sky would look very different and might indeed be quite unsuitable for the shots you had planned on a dull day when the sea appeared grey and there were no highlights and only weak shadows. Unless you are prepared to arrange with your model to cancel the session and try again it is always worth while looking for an alternative location or for other backgrounds you can use in the place you have selected. Although grey sea and sky can look effective when shooting in black-and-white or when a particular mood is required, for colour shots as a general rule they will not be very pleasing and you will need to find settings that will introduce some additional contrast either tonally or in terms of colour. A brightly painted doorway or

wall could give a lift to the pictures when shooting in colour, or areas of very light or dark tones included in the picture area to increase the brightness range when shooting in black-and-white.

The setting can also have a considerable influence on the quality and nature of the lighting; a woodland scene, for example, can create quite considerable contrast even on a dull day because of the shadows produced by trees and foliage whereas an open sandy beach will produce a

Privacy and ease of access are vital considerations when choosing a location for nude photography.

CHOOSING A LOCATION 2

great deal of reflected light and reduce the brightness range even in bright sunlight. These effects will also affect the mood of a picture so the lighting potential of a setting should be considered in terms of mood as well as quality. Sunlight, for instance, may well be inappropriate for the pictures you want to take and your choice of setting may be dictated partly by the need to find areas of shade for your shots. Low light levels are often conducive to the establishment of mood and atmosphere and settings which can be used in this way can be very effective, whether the effect is created simply by the shade of a leafy wood or a building or by making use of low levels of daylight such as a sunset or at dusk in an urban setting where artifical lighting can be incorporated into the picture.

Each setting has its own particular lighting conditions which will influence both the quality and mood of a picture. In this respect a beach location is very different from a woodland, and due allowance must be made when shooting.

BEACHES 1

A beach is understandably one of the most popular locations for nude photography and for a variety of reasons. In the first place it provides a logic for nudity as many pictures of the nude are unsuccessful quite simply because the model looks out of place in the setting that has been chosen. The technique whereby unusual locations are used to create a dramatic or ambiguous effect needs to be approached very carefully since the results can only too easily look silly, but this is unlikely to happen with pictures taken in a beach setting. In addition a beach provides a natural and relaxed environment for the model, one in which she is less likely to feel restricted or inhibited and to which she will be able to relate more easily; this makes such a location ideally suited to the more inexperienced model or photographer.

Another reason why a beach is a good choice for nude pictures is that the quality of the light can be particularly pleasing and flattering. This is especially true in conditions of bright sunlight where in less reflective surroundings such light can easily create excessive contrast. The large amount of light reflected from the light-toned sand and sea will tend to make the choice of viewpoint and camera angle less restricted on a beach than it would be in a setting with darker, more enclosed surroundings. This can, however, create its own problems: exposure readings can, for example, be quite misleading since the scattered light can cause a meter to indicate unrealistically high readings and great care must be taken to avoid underexposure. The safest method is to take very close-up readings from an important mid-tone in the subject, and this is necessary even when quite long shots are taken.

When using a camera with TTL metering a zoom lens can be useful in this respect since the reading can be taken with the zoom extended and then retracted for the exposures. With a tripod-mounted camera a hand meter will be an advantage as close-up readings can be taken from the model without disturbing the camera, and the incident light facility of most hand meters can also be an effective way of taking readings under difficult conditions.

As well as exposure problems the colour quality of light by the sea also needs consideration as it tends to be of a higher colour temperature and there is a greater presence of ultra-violet light. Both these factors will tend to create a blue cast when shooting in colour and in general you will need to use a warm filter in the order of 81A or 81B to compensate; this will also be necessary when shooting in open shade or against the light with a blue sky. A polarizing filter is often invaluable in beach settings as it can be used to control some of the scattered and reflected light, thus creating richer tones and colours as well as making the sky darker blue and the sea more translucent.

In addition to the visual properties the physical qualities of a beach are an important element in nude photography. Water in particular can be a valuable asset since skin and water together have both strong textural and sensual properties that can add considerable impact to a picture. The effect of water on the model's skin is often heightened by the use of a little oil; if this is rubbed in well the water will form into well-defined droplets and of course the skin itself will also look more lustrous. Shots of this type can be taken with the model actually in the water so that she can constantly dip under the surface causing the water to run

*The higher colour temperature of the light in a seaside location has to be taken into consideration when shooting. In both these pictures, one taken early in the day (**left**) and the other at late evening (**opposite**), an 81 filter was used to warm up the subject, with fill-in flash to compensate for the shadows.*

BEACHES 2

off her skin in rivulets. Where there is a suitable surf she can also lie in the edge of the water so that the waves flow over her; this can be an ideal situation in which to experiment with slow shutter speeds with the camera mounted on a tripod to create a wispy, smoke-like quality in moving water, whereas with the model dipping under the water a fast shutter speed will be more effective in recording the individual droplets of spray.

Water on skin is an effective subject for the more abstract or close-up approach and for this it may be more convenient to have the model positioned on dry land and to apply the water by spraying it or flicking it on to her body. As a general rule such pictures are more successful with dark or tanned skin although a paler skin can be made to look more appealing with a little contrivance. A pale skin should be well oiled and a warm filter such as an 81B used, indirect light is best either by shooting in open shade or into the light, and a degree of under-exposure will heighten the textural quality of the image; in some circumstances a polarizing filter will also help to improve the skin tone. In addition to indirect light a very low, late-afternoon sunlight acutely angled so that it literally skims across the surface of the skin can also be effective in revealing texture. Care is needed, however, as directional sunlight can create an unflattering effect, and in these conditions you will be unlikely to need the warm filter because the light will have a lower colour temperature at this time of the day.

To add another dimension to shots taken in a beach location look out for elements other than just the sand and water – fishing boats, driftwood, rocks and small pools can all be very effective and will give your pictures more interest – and if you can find a quiet enough spot the usual trappings of holiday resorts such as deckchairs and beach huts can add both colour and variety. You should also consider the practical problems of shooting on a beach. Sand and seawater are extremely harmful to camera equipment and you must be very careful to protect them. Store individual items in plastic bags inside your camera case and remove all traces of sand and water before replacing them after use; flick or blow sand away from the surface before wiping and be especially careful with lenses and glass surfaces. Do not forget the model's needs and comfort: plan your location and shots so that she has a chance to maintain both her composure and her hair and make-up throughout the day, and leave the wet or sandy shots until after the other shots have been taken.

(**Far left**) An 81A filter was used to compensate for the overcast day in this shot taken in subdued light. (**Left**) A combination of flash and a very fast speed of 1/400 sec was used to freeze the surf in this action-filled picture. (**Below**) An 81A filter added warmth to the subject and fill-in flash was used to compensate for the early-morning shadows.

VILLAS AND SWIMMING POOLS 1

Like a beach, a villa or a swimming pool provides a believable setting for nude pictures with the added advantage that there is a much greater degree of comfort and privacy. However, much more depends on the actual physical appearance of the setting for the outcome of the session, and in general the backgrounds and settings will be more restricted unless you are fortunate enough to have access to a really opulent villa. Another advantage is that in the event of bad or unsuitable weather you will be able to consider interior locations and even for the exterior shots there will always be a readily available stock of props and accessories. This type of location will of course produce pictures with a quite different quality from those taken in a natural setting as the backgrounds will be harder and more angular. In general this will be the main advantage of this type of location and the way you see and approach your pictures should reflect this aspect. A wide-angle lens is often an advantage since when combined with the closer and more restricted viewpoints it will enable you to emphasize the effect of perspective and exaggerate the lines and shapes created by the setting. In addition to the wider backgrounds provided by the location you will also be able to find small corners which can be used effectively for closer shots – a mosaic tiled surround, for instance, or a shuttered door or window, even an angled white wall combined with perhaps an interesting shadow or a flowering plant could provide the finishing touch to a picture.

The swimming pool will also have some useful applications since shots of the model in the water are often much easier to control when she is in a pool than in the sea, and it is possible to use more interesting and varied viewpoints, for example shooting down on to the model from the diving board. Another advantage is that most pools have an almost luminously coloured lining which can make the water appear a more attractive colour than the sea in some circumstances, particularly when the sea is rough or the sky is cloudy. This can create a problem, however, as it can easily create a colour cast by reflecting light on to the model, and you need to take care in choosing model positions and camera angles. Like a beach setting a villa location usually has very bright reflective surroundings such as white walls and this can mean that exposure readings must be taken with care. However, because of the greater number of angles and shadows in a villa setting the brightness range and contrast can be much more pronounced than on a beach. You will need to choose viewpoints and model positions carefully to avoid excessive contrast, and quite often reflectors or fill-in flash will be necessary to control the contrast. The harsh quality of such a setting in bright sunlight can, however, be used as a positive element by deliberately allowing areas of the picture to be burnt out or lost in shadow. Photographers like Helmut Newton have often used these harsh and dramatic qualities very effectively in their pictures.

A villa offers a variety of potential settings for nude work. Doorways and windows provide effective angles and frames for the image, while the textures of walls and woodwork add further interest.

VILLAS AND SWIMMING POOLS 2

A swimming pool has a number of advantages over a beach location. Privacy is assured, shots of the model in the pool are easier to control and the colour of the water is usually more attractive than that of the sea.

IN THE CITY

As far as nude photography is concerned, an urban location is, generally speaking, used rather less frequently, partly because it does not provide a logic in the same way that a beach or villa setting does, and partly because the problem of finding quiet and private settings is that much greater. However, it does lend itself to this genre in perhaps a more limited way – like a villa setting, a city-scape provides the more dramatic and contrived quality of manmade structures, and when used with sensitivity can create unusual and even surreal effects in a picture. The main problems with shots of this type are almost entirely practical ones: how to find locations that are interesting and urban enough to make them worth using, but at the same time private enough to avoid crowds of onlookers or, worse still, official intervention. One obvious solution is to choose the time of day with care – even the busiest parts of a city are largely devoid of people at six o'clock in the morning, for example, or on a Sunday, and when you are planning to take shots in a fairly public place this will be the only answer. There are other solutions, however, such as locating private places within the urban setting and obtaining the necessary permission to shoot there, in an industrial area, for example, or in a private garden or park. Another solution is to find a house or apartment that has a suitable outlook for use as a background: photographers like Helmut Newton and Jeff Dunas often use balconies or rooftop terraces in this way.

A town or city setting can provide scope for striking pictures, especially in the context of nude photography. It is important to ensure, however, that you will not be infringing any byelaws before you start shooting.

NIGHT SHOTS

The majority of photographers
restrict their picture-taking
outdoors to the daytime, but it is
possible to create successful
images after the sun has gone
down. The use of flash in a night
shot produces an interesting
effect (**left**). In the two pictures
shot at sunset, the use of flash
illuminates the models fully
(**opposite**), while shooting
without flash produces a
silhouette effect (**below**).

MOODY SETTINGS 1

Mood is a very subjective quality in a picture, and the photographer who wishes to impart a particular mood must depend largely on his own taste and instinct when choosing a setting. Elements such as lighting, colour and image quality will also have a marked effect, but when a picture is taken within a setting it will be that factor that has the most dominant influence. This can be seen very easily from the work of photographers like Helmut Newton, David Hamilton and Jeff Dunas where the choice of location is almost an inherent part of their style and approach. Mood is most readily created in a photograph when something is left to the imagination – a picture which is well lit, sharp and clear and in which all the details are boldly defined is not likely to convey much impression of mood or atmosphere – and this should be taken into account when choosing a location. Avoid settings with a lot of fussy detail and instead look for places where there are soft and subtle tones and colours and where there is a quality of light and colour that will be in keeping with the mood you wish to portray.

Tone and colour are vital factors in the creation of mood; a setting that contains predominantly dark, shadowy tones and details, for instance, will enable you to shoot low-key pictures which will help to establish a more subdued or sombre mood, whereas a light-toned setting will lend itself to high-key images with a more gentle and romantic atmosphere. A setting with bold, bright, fully saturated colours will create a similarly bright and cheerful mood, while soft, pastel colours in a scene will produce a lighter, more whimsical mood, and darker, neutral hues will be more suited to pictures with a more serious or even sad atmosphere. It is important to appreciate as well that the predominant colour quality of a setting will also affect the mood of a picture: red, orange and yellow tend to create a warm and inviting quality, blues and greens suggest a more peaceful and relaxed mood, while at the other end of the spectrum indigo and violet can impart a more introspective or dramatic atmosphere.

In a more general way you should consider the relevance of the setting to the mood you are trying to achieve; for example, a rustic farmhouse interior of the type favoured by David Hamilton would not lend itself very well to either the models or the type of mood preferred by a photographer like Helmut Newton. It must be appreciated that the mood of a photograph will result from the successful combination of a number of different factors – the model, clothes and accessories, lighting, colour and tonal quality as well as the setting – and each must be considered in relation to the other, as if one of them is inappropriate then the over-all effect will invariably be to destroy the mood.

The use of infra-red film with a sepia filter has produced the warm, vibrant mood in this shot.

The choice of a particular setting will influence the mood of a picture. In these two examples the exotic outdoor location immediately conjures up a relaxed, expansive mood.

MOODY SETTINGS 2

The tones and colours of an image are important factors in the creation of mood: strong, bright colours produce a bold, vigorous effect, while softer, pastel hues have a gentler quality.

COMPOSITION

While the question of composition for studio pictures is largely one of selecting a background and positioning the model, in outdoor pictures the approach tends to be far less restricted, partly because an outdoor location provides a greater variety of opportunities and also because there is a much wider choice of camera viewpoint. The major factors in composition are the choice of viewpoint, the position of the model, the way the image is framed and the choice of lens; by combining these elements, a wide variety of possibilities is opened up within each situation. In its simplest form, a nude picture would consist only of subject and background, and in many photographs the background will be a fairly negative quality, merely providing a contrasting tone or colour so that the model is clearly defined; in many ways this is the outdoor equivalent of a roll of background paper in the studio. However, it is often far more effective to use the background or setting in a more defined and dominant way, especially if you wish to create a mood or to introduce more interest into the image, and it is in this context that the choice of viewpoint and the framing of the picture become more important.

In the majority of nude pictures the model will be the centre of interest in the image and for this reason she should always be placed in the strongest position within the frame. This can be achieved in two ways: by choosing where she is to stand and by framing the picture with care. A human figure tends to attract the eye wherever it is placed, particularly a nude figure, and for this reason it can often be quite small in relation to the setting. However, if the picture is to be well balanced and composed it is important that other details and objects are placed within the frame in such a way that they are of secondary importance and are not allowed to be distracting or to create an imbalance in the image. Tones and colours must be considered in the same way – a bright highlight, for example, or a bold colour which occurs unplanned in the background of a picture can be just as unwelcome as a distracting detail or object. When framing the picture it is important to study the image carefully within the viewfinder to ensure that you can see all the details in relation to each other and to experiment with different ways of positioning the frame until the best balance is achieved.

The choice of viewpoint is another vital factor in the composition of a picture and you should learn to explore all the possibilities that this can offer before starting to shoot. A more distant viewpoint, for example, will allow you to include more in the frame and will also alter the perspective between subject and background. In addition, it can enable you to include foreground details to add interest or to increase the impression of depth in the image. A higher or lower viewpoint can also have a significant effect on the composition, and this is often a way of creating more impact in a picture. The important thing about composition is to allow your own instincts and taste to decide these factors, as this is the best way to develop a personal style. Do not always choose the safe or obvious option but have the courage sometimes to go against the rules and to experiment with new ideas.

The model may dominate the composition of a nude picture, with the background merely providing a contrasting tone **(above left)**, *or the background may play a greater role in creating atmosphere* **(above right)**.

Careful framing and harmonious colours have produced a well-balanced composition in this tropical grove.

CALENDAR SESSION

The shoot for an important calendar project on location involves a great deal of time, money and effort. Choosing the right models requires careful casting and test sessions, and a reconnaissance trip is usually made beforehand to find suitable settings and backgrounds. In addition to the photographer and models themselves, the trip will usually include a stylist, make-up artist and art director, and perhaps a representative from the client company.

APRIL

		M	A	R		
M	T	W	T	F	S	S
30	31					1
2	3	4	5	6	7	8
9	10	11	12	13	14	15
16	17	18	19	20	21	22
23	24	25	26	27	28	29

		A	P	R		
M	T	W	T	F	S	S
		1	2	3	4	5
6	7	8	9	10	11	12
13	14	15	16	17	18	19
20	21	22	23	24	25	26
27	28	29	30			

		M	A	Y		
M	T	W	T	F	S	S
				1	2	3
4	5	6	7	8	9	10
11	12	13	14	15	16	17
18	19	20	21	22	23	24
25	26	27	28	29	30	31

Today
Long haul, short haul, in motorway
or on off road applications, the
Dunlop truck tyre range gives proven
performance with economy.

SHOOTING IN SUNLIGHT 1

It is only natural that most people prefer to shoot pictures when the sun is shining, and it does have some advantages – indeed in some situations it is almost a necessity – yet sunlight does create a few problems and has to be approached with some care. Direct sunlight can easily be unflattering, emphasizing skin texture and creating a harsh quality with dense shadows. When used in this way, the position of the model and the viewpoint must be chosen with care to avoid these effects: the angle of the model's head, for instance, should be placed so that the light falls on it from an angle which creates only small shadows. When the sun is quite high in the sky you must be careful to avoid shadows forming under the eyes and dense shadows under the chin; this can sometimes be avoided by asking the model to tilt her head up towards the sunlight, although this might make her squint and frown, which creates its own problems. As a general rule, when direct sunlight is wanted for a shot it is best to shoot later or earlier in the day when the sun is lower in the sky. This has the added advantage that the sunlight at this time is a little more mellow in both quality and colour.

It is also important to appreciate that direct sunlight can easily create a brightness range that is greater than the film can record, resulting in excessive contrast with either dense, blocked-up shadows or bleached-out highlights. One solution is to choose a camera and model position that either gives only very small areas of shadow or means that the model is primarily in shadow, and to calculate the exposure accordingly. A better solution is to use a reflector placed close to the model on the shadow side and angled to deflect the sunlight back into the shadows, thus reducing their density and the contrast. A small flash-gun can also be used to fill in the shadows. The method in this case is to calculate the correct exposure for the highlight areas of the subject and then to select an aperture that will give between one and two stops under-exposure for the flash; if you give the full exposure for the flash the shadows will be completely eliminated and this will appear unnatural. Although direct sunlight is often desirable and can be effective with longer shots, a more close-up picture often requires a softer light, and in these circumstances it is necessary to find some way of diffusing or reflecting the sunlight. One method is to use a large diffusion screen made of either white translucent nylon or tracing paper supported on a frame and positioned between the sun and the model; this will obviously have to be quite large for anything but head-and-shoulders pictures. If you are able to move the model the simplest solution is to position her within an area of open shade such as under a tree or in the shade of a wall. When there is a blue sky, however, this will tend to create a blue cast when shooting in colour and it will usually be necessary to use an 81A or 81B filter to correct the effect.

*Shooting in sunlight brings both advantages and disadvantages, and due care must be taken. At midday when the direct sunlight creates a harsh quality, reflectors can be used to fill in the shadows and give less contrast (**above and top**). An alternative is to shoot very early in the day when the light has a softer quality (**opposite**).*

SHOOTING IN SUNLIGHT 2

(**Opposite**) In this shot taken in shadow at midday, fill-in flash was used to retain detail in the shadow area. (**Left**) Here, a reflector was placed at the front of the model to bounce the light back from outside the cave. The exposure was calculated for the model, leaving the rest to over-expose. (**Below**) The shadows were allowed to go dark in this midday nude study. The exposure was calculated for the highlights to create a deliberately contrasty effect.

SHOOTING IN SOFT DAYLIGHT

In a purely technical sense a hazy or even slightly cloudy day is preferable for nude photography because the atmosphere creates a natural diffusion which reduces the density of the shadows cast by the sun and produces lower contrast. In these circumstances the brightness range is likely to be within the range of the film without the need for reflectors or fill-in flash. It is still necessary, however, to consider the position and density of the shadows in terms of the effect they create – on a very overcast day, for example, an excessively top light effect can be created very noticeably with facial lighting, with unpleasant shadow under the eyes and chin. The solution is similar to that used when shooting in sunlight, asking the model to tilt her head upwards, for example, or using a white or silver reflector placed close to and under her face to reflect the light up into these areas. Another solution is to position the model so that the top light is screened from her, making the over-all lighting effect more frontal, under a tree for example, or in a doorway.

As the softer light of a cloudy day is much less directional it will tend to give you greater freedom in the choice of viewpoint and model position, but when the day is very overcast the brightness range can be reduced to a point where there is insufficient contrast in the image and the pictures can appear flat and dull. The simplest way of overcoming this is to compose your shots so that more contrast is introduced into the subject either in terms of tones or colours. With a colour shot, for example, you could add contrast to the picture by introducing some red or yellow clothes or accessories into the shot, and in black-and-white shots you could add light-toned props or accessories and position your model against a dark tone in the background, or vice versa. It is possible to use flash to increase the lighting contrast as well as to reduce it, but for full-length shots it will need to be quite powerful. The procedure is to set the aperture of the camera to give the correct exposure for the flash and to select a shutter speed that will under-expose the daylight exposure by between one and two stops; in this way the flash becomes the main or key light and the daylight acts as a fill-in.

Shooting in soft light on an overcast day is particularly effective for nude photography. In this moody colour shot taken at midday, a reflector was used to the left of the model to reflect light on to her body, and her red skirt introduces contrast into the picture (right).

Using a fair-skinned model is an effective way of creating contrast when the lighting is subdued (**below**), while shooting with the model in shadow can produce a pleasingly soft quality (**left**).

AGAINST THE LIGHT

One approach to shooting in daylight which is particularly effective with nude photography is to shoot towards the sun; with the sun behind the model this has the effect of using the light reflected from the sky, which is of course diffused, as the main source. This has a number of advantages. One is that this softer light will create a more flattering effect which enhances skin quality, another is that in many instances it will create a pleasing halo of light around the outline of the model, and it can also subdue unwanted or distracting background details. There are, however, a number of problems with this lighting approach. Exposure calculation can be rather less straightforward than in normal circumstances because the image will contain extremely bright highlights, and if a reading is made in the ordinary way, taking an average from the whole of the subject, the picture will usually be underexposed. The best method is to take a close-up reading from a mid-tone in the subject, usually from the model, being careful to screen the meter from the background or highlight areas, or alternatively to take an incident reading. If neither of these methods is practical then you must increase the exposure indicated by a normal averaging reading by one and a half to two stops. Another problem is that shooting into the sun can create a blue cast as the subject is being lit primarily by light reflected from a blue sky and so it is usually necessary to use an 81A or 81B filter. This type of lighting will also of course create an extremely high brightness range, but in many cases the areas of highlight will be very small and of little importance and the loss of detail as a result of over-exposure can often simply be ignored. In other circumstances you will need to use either fill-in flash or reflectors to reduce the contrast.

*Shooting against the light creates a number of different effects: the background is burnt out (**top**), back-lighting (**above**), back-lighting in evening light will fill-in flash (**left**), back-lighting with a gold reflector (**opposite**).*

COLOUR AND DAYLIGHT

When shooting in daylight it is important to be fully aware of how the quality of the light affects the colour rendering of the film. This is particularly important with nude photography because the flesh tones which are all-important in this type of work are extremely sensitive to even slight shifts in the colour balance of the film. The colour temperature of daylight can vary quite considerably depending upon the time of day and the atmosphere; daylight colour transparency film is balanced for use with light at approximately 5500° Kelvin and variations in the colour temperature will produce a significant colour cast on the film even though it might not be apparent to the eye. The colour temperature of daylight decreases when the sun is lower in the sky in the morning and evening; this will create a warm or orange cast on the film and can be corrected by the use of a bluish filter such as an 82A, 82B or 82C. There are more situations, however, in which the colour temperature can be much higher than that for which the film is balanced, thus producing a blue cast on the film. The most common are when the sky is overcast, at high altitudes or near the sea when the ultra-violet content of the light is much greater, and when shooting against the light or in open shade on a sunny day. In these circumstances it is necessary to use the orange-tinted filters in the range of 81A, 81B or 81C. As a general rule, a slight warm cast is more acceptable with skin tones and in some cases can improve the effect of a shot, while a blue cast, on the other hand, is usually unwelcome since it can make skin appear rather cold and waxy. Consequently, if you suspect that the colour temperature might be too high then it is generally best to use a warm filter to be safe. In addition to the actual colour temperature of the daylight its general quality will also have an important effect on the colour in the image. As a general rule, bright colours in the subject will be enhanced when the light is quite soft and diffused, while a hard, directional light will create highlights and dense shadows which will degrade the colours and detract from their effect. In these circumstances a hazy day or shooting in open shade or against the light is preferable to shooting in direct sunlight.

*The colour temperature of daylight varies considerably throughout the day, and this must be taken into account when shooting. In this location shot in front of a villa (**right**), taken in evening light which catches the model's face, a gold reflector was used to add warmth and to enhance the richness of the door and the model's skirt. In conditions where the ultra-violet content of the light is high, such as by the sea (**opposite**), an 81A filter can be used to enrichen the skin tones.*

USE OF COLOUR

A good understanding of how colour film responds to the colours in a subject and how colour can be used to best effect in a picture is a vital skill for any photographer, but in the nude medium the photographer has a great deal more control over this particular element of his pictures than in the field of landscape photography, for instance, and so this knowledge is if anything even more important if he is to make the best of his opportunities. Colour transparency film is designed to give a correct result under quite precise lighting conditions and if this varies the colour quality of the result will not be true. Daylight colour film, for example, is intended for use with a light source of a colour temperature of about 5500° Kelvin which approximates to that of noon sunlight; when the colour temperature is much higher than this, say on a dull day or in open shade, the resulting picture will have a blue cast, and when the colour temperature is lower, around sunset or when shooting in artificial light, the picture will have an orange cast. Even quite small variations that are not apparent to the naked eye will produce a noticeable colour cast: film that is designed for use with tungsten studio lights, for example, will produce a warm or orange cast when used with ordinary domestic bulbs because these are of a slightly higher colour temperature.

This question of the colour temperature of the light source is vital to the photographer of the nude as he is dealing principally with skin tones and these are particularly indicative of variations in colour quality, and even a slight blue cast, for instance, will give the flesh tones an unpleasant quality. A colour temperature meter is available which measures the colour quality of the light source in the same way that an exposure meter measures the level of brightness, but in most cases it is possible to anticipate those situations in which a colour cast might occur or to judge them visually and to use the appropriate colour correction filter. The most commonly used range of correction filters are the 81 and 82 series; the 81A, 81B and 81C are very pale orange tinted filters of progressively greater density which can be used to warm up the image when the colour temperature of the light source is too high, and the 82A, 82B and 82C are bluish filters which can be used to cool the colour quality when the colour temperature is too low. These precautions are really only necessary when shooting with colour transparency film as with colour negative film variations in the colour quality can be adjusted by filtration at the printing stage, but since the majority of pictures of this type are taken on transparency film it must be taken into account.

Just as important as the colour quality of the image is the colour content, and the way in which colour is used and distributed in the picture will have a marked effect on both the mood and the composition of the picture. The colour content of an image has such a dominant effect that it can easily override other aspects of the composition and so when shooting in colour it is vital to consider the most effective way of using it; when a picture contains

bold areas of colour, for example, these will attract the eye so strongly that unless they are part of, or close to, the main centre of interest of the picture they will become a distraction. Similarly, in a picture that contains a number of bright colours distributed throughout the image the effect will be one of discord and conflict even if the picture is well composed in other respects. The most effective way of using colour in a photograph is to restrict it to just one or two bright colours, with the remainder of the picture either in contrast or as a quite neutral hue. This is particularly important when the colours are bright and fully saturated; with softer and more harmonious colours the effect is not as marked. Fortunately, in nude photography it is possible in most circumstances to control the colour content of the picture quite strictly either by the choice of clothes, props and backgrounds or by the position chosen for the model and the camera viewpoint and the way the picture is framed, and these factors should be used to ensure that the colours are selected and positioned to create the most telling effect. They can be chosen to create a bold effect – for example, a dark-skinned model wearing a yellow leotard and placed against a dark-toned background would have a very striking effect even though there was only one main colour in the picture – or alternatively, the colours could be selected so that they blended and harmonized to create a more subtle and romantic effect like the pale pinks and blues of a photograph by David Hamilton.

*It is possible to shoot at midday in shadow, using reflectors and fill-in flash, and still retain the colours in an image (**above**). In the rustic interior shot*

*(**opposite**) the gold and brown of the model's outfit is conveyed by the use of part daylight and part fill-in flash.*

COLOUR AND MOOD

A photographer should be aware of how the colours in a subject can be controlled in order to create the most effective composition, but at the same time he should appreciate how the colour quality of an image will affect the mood of a picture. Each of the colours in the spectrum has its own 'mood' value and the presence of a particular colour in a picture will therefore contribute this aspect to the over-all effect. Red, for instance, is a very bold and assertive colour which will tend to dominate other aspects of the image; when used as a contrasting hue it will usually create a quite dramatic and lively effect in the picture. The same is true of orange and yellow, though to a rather lesser extent. Blues and greens have a more restful, peaceful quality and will help to create pictures with a more gentle or romantic mood, while the more sombre hues of indigo and violet will tend to produce a more serious or intro-spective atmosphere.

The way that the colours in a picture react with each other will also affect the mood. Colours which harmonize will tend to create a quieter, less vigorous quality while colours which create a contrast or a discord in the image will produce a more dominant or cheerful mood. In the same way bright, fully saturated colours will also tend to create a bold or lively quality while dark, sombre colours or pastel hues will help to produce pictures of a more restrained and atmospheric nature.

Colour and mood are closely related in every image. In these two pictures, the dramatic quality of late-afternoon sunlight has produced a warm, vibrant effect (right), while the blues and greens have created a more restful mood (opposite).

SOFT COLOUR EFFECTS

The use of soft colours can be particularly appropriate to nude photography, partly because as a general rule they tend to create a more flattering image as far as the model is concerned but also because they are often more effective in the production of pictures with a definite mood or atmosphere. The most immediate means of achieving soft colour effects is by a careful and judicious choice of the model's clothes and accessories and the selection of an appropriate background tone, and also by the way in which the picture is framed. In this way it is possible to ensure that the image contains only colours from a similar area of the spectrum and that contrasting hues are excluded. There are, however, other factors which will also affect this soft colour quality in a picture. While it is possible to create a soft effect when the colours are saturated, providing they harmonize, desaturated or pastel hues will be far more effective in producing really soft and romantic images. Lighting is important in this respect – for instance, a diffused light which creates quite soft-edged shadows and produces a fairly low brightness range in the subject will be more effective in emphasizing soft colours than a hard directional light. In outdoor situations on a sunny day this can be arranged by placing the model in open shade or by shooting into the sun. This method has the added advantage that it can on occasions be used to create a degree of controlled flare which can cause considerable desaturation of the colours as well as a lowering of image contrast, especially when combined with over-exposure.

A degree of over-exposure can be used to create softer colours in other circumstances, and with subjects that have a low brightness range under-exposure can also be exploited to make colours less saturated and harmonize more readily with each other. In addition to exposure techniques soft focus attachments and fog or pastel filters can create soft colour effects, given the right subject. When shooting in outdoor locations where background colours are obtrusive, it is often possible to make these softer by means of differential focusing; by placing the model some distance from the background and using a wide aperture, preferably with a long-focus lens, the background will be thrown so far out of focus that the colours will blend to create a softer effect. The same principle can of course also be applied to foreground details.

Soft colours usually produce a flattering effect, which is especially desirable in nude work. In outdoor locations, background colours can be softened by differential focusing which throws them out of focus (right).

*Pastel colours, like those in this sun-bleached background, are particularly effective in the production of a soft image (**above**)*

EXPOSURE

In nude photography, where the aim is to create a mood rather than a strictly factual record, the exposure can be calculated to achieve the desired effect. The exposure can be taken for the highlight tones to give detail in the texture of the model's skin (**below**), or a slight degree of under-exposure can be used to make the colours richer and stronger (**far right**). By taking the exposure from the model in the shadow area (**right**), both the background and the sun-lit foreground are over-exposed, giving a delicate effect. For the beach shot (**opposite**), taken in early morning light, the exposure is calculated for the model, with fill-in flash to balance the shadows.

FILTERS 1

There are basically two categories of filters for use when shooting in colour: correction filters that are used to adjust the balance between the colour temperature of the light source and that of the film in use, and effects filters which are used to introduce a deliberate colour cast into the image in order to alter the mood or colour quality of a picture. While strong correction filters are available that will enable daylight film to be used with tungsten light and vice versa, for instance, in most circumstances correction filters are used to correct smaller differences in colour temperature. The most useful filters for nude work are those in the 81 range A-B-C which create a progressively warmer effect to correct the blue cast which can result from shooting on overcast days, in open shade, into the light and near the sea or in the mountains when ultra-violet light can be more predominant. The UV filter is an almost colourless filter that will help to correct the effects of ultra-violet light but will in general not be strong enough when the light is of a substantially higher colour temperature than that for which the film is balanced. However, as the UV filter will have no adverse effect on the image when it is not required many photographers simply leave it on the lens permanently, because it offers some protection to the front element of the lens. The 80 and 82 ranges of filters have a pale blue tint and can be used to correct the warm cast that will be created when the light source is of a lower colour temperature than that for which the film is balanced. This occurs in shooting when the sun is low in the sky or shooting in ordinary domestic lighting with artificial light film which is balanced for use with photographic lamps which have a higher colour temperature.

All of these filters can be used for creating a colour cast when a special effect is needed, but in addition there is also a series of filters available in acetate in both the primary and secondary colours in a wide range of densities that can be mixed to create a specific hue. These can be placed in a special holder which is fitted on to the lens like an ordinary filter. When shooting in black-and-white, filters can create a tonal contrast between the colours in a subject: if a filter of the same colour as a particular object in a scene is fitted over the lens it will make that object record as a lighter tone on the print, while colours of an opposite hue will record as a darker tone. A girl wearing a blue dress standing in front of a red door, for instance, would photograph with the dress and the door of similar tones in a black-and-white print when shot without a filter but a red filter would make the dress appear as a much darker tone and the door as a much lighter tone; a blue filter would reverse this and produce a dark-toned door with a light-toned dress.

*A star-burst filter was used to create the burst of light from the highlight on the water (**below**). A polarizing filter eliminates some of the light reflected from shiny surfaces; in this picture (**bottom**) it has made the water more translucent and richer. In this sunset shot (**opposite**), a 20 red filter was used to add warmth to the image, with fill-in flash to balance the detail.*

FILTERS 2

In the two pictures above, both shot in open shade, the left-hand picture was taken without a filter, which has resulted in a slightly blue cast, while the other was taken with an 81B filter which restores the warm skin tones. An 81A filter was used in the beach shot (**opposite**) to create a warm effect, with a polarizing filter to reduce the reflections from the wet fabric and the water and to produce richer colours.

The illustration (**right**) shows the colour temperature of various familiar light sources, from candlelight to shade under a blue sky. As the colour temperature of the light source increases, it creates a bluer cast on the film which requires a yellowish filter to correct it; as the temperature decreases, it creates a red cast which requires a blue filter.

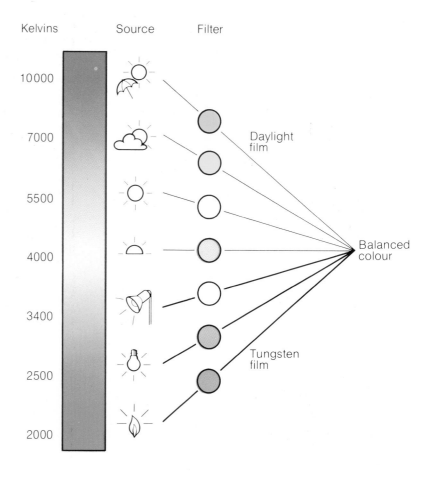

LENSES

A long-focus lens, used from a distant viewpoint, has isolated a small detail of the figure and compressed the perspective (**below**). The use of a wide-angle lens (**bottom**) has emphasized the effect of a high viewpoint and exaggerated the perspective, making the model's legs appear longer. A 180 mm lens, used for the 6 x 7 cm format (**right**), has given less depth of field, causing the background to go out of focus.

INSTANT CAMERA

Instant film is extremely useful for checking the composition and lighting of an image in order to improve the final result (**right**).

POST-CAMERA 1

Once the film has been exposed there are still a wide variety of techniques which can be used to create different effects and qualities in the image. The home darkroom worker has many advantages in this respect as even basic processing and printing offer considerable control over the final photograph in comparison to trade processing in both black-and-white and colour. Perhaps the most basic form of image manipulation is contrast control with black-and-white pictures. Quite dramatic effects can be created by printing negatives on to a harder grade of paper than would normally be used; this has the effect of producing bold, stark images in which the tonal masses of the image and the shapes and lines of the subject are emphasized and the more subtle gradations of the picture are lost. While this can be very dramatic when conventional bromide papers of Grades 3, 4 and 5 are used, even more unusual pictures can be produced by the use of Lith materials (this is a film that when processed in the specially formulated developer will convert a normal graduated image into one with only black-and-white tones). The point at which the image divides into black or white is determined by the exposure so that a short exposure will record only the darkest tones as black with the rest of the picture as pure white, while a longer exposure will record all but the lightest tones as black. These materials can also be used to create tone separations or posterized images. The principle is to make two Lith positives from a normal black-and-white negative, one very light so that only the shadows record and one very dark with only the highlights as clear film. These are both printed in register on to the same sheet of normal negative film, and the result will be a negative which will produce a print consisting of just three tones: black, white and a mid-grey. The Lith positives can also be used to print on to colour transparency film using different colour filters for each exposure to create a wide range of effects. More tones and colours can be produced by making more than two Lith positives from the original, each of course of different densities.

Another way of creating an image with an unusual tonal range is by solarization (more accurately called the Sabbatier effect). This involves re-exposing a negative about half-way through the development and continuing for the normal time. The result is an image which is partially negative and partially positive, with a fine line outlining the tonal masses. The degree of re-exposure required is quite small and you will have to experiment to determine the exact amount; for this reason it is unwise to attempt this technique with original negatives and copies should be made first. The resulting image can be quite soft and it can therefore be an advantage to make the copy negatives on Lith film but processed in a conventional developer.

A texture screen is an effective way of producing a picture with a different quality. In this technique, a film image of a textured surface such as hessian is placed in contact with the negative and a print made from the combination. Ready-made texture screens can be bought from photographic dealers but it can be more interesting to make your own by photographing a variety of surfaces. If you choose essentially dark objects or under-expose to make a weak image you can use the resulting negative as the texture screen. In addition to an image on film it is also possible to use translucent paper or fabric – the material used for negative sleeves can produce a very pleasing granular effect, for example – and instead of placing the texture screen in contact with the negative a larger piece can be used and placed in contact with the printing paper during the exposure.

Montaging is a technique which the darkroom worker can use to produce a multiple image; it is similar in principle to double exposure in the camera but uses two or more negatives printed on to the same sheet of paper. As it is carried out under more controlled conditions and the exposures can be varied at will and shading and dodging techniques used when printing, it is possible to

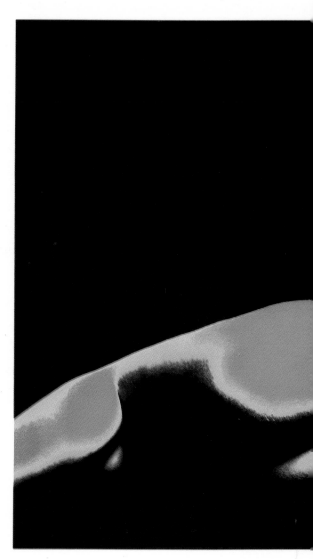

Home-made texture screens can produce interesting textural effects. In this picture (**above left**) a piece of translucent paper was sandwiched with the negative and a print made from the combination. In a tone separation (**above right**) three Lith positives are used to create an image with just three tones of white, grey and black. Solarization is a method of creating unusual tones in an image; in this example (**left**) the effect was produced by a chemical toning process and then colour-dyeing the result.

POST-CAMERA 2

have much more control over this technique than with a double exposure in the camera. Having selected the negatives you wish to use it is best to make an initial sketch of the final image, bearing in mind that when printing from negatives you will need to juxtapose the darker tones of one image against the lighter tones of another for them to be clearly defined; a semi-silhouetted nude figure could be montaged very effectively on to a light-toned seascape or cloud formation, for example. The next stage is to take a piece of drawing paper of the size you intend to make your print and place this in the masking frame. Then size up and focus the first of the negatives and make a tracing of its main outlines on the paper; you can now make a test strip in the normal way to determine the right exposure. Replace this first negative with the next and size, focus and position the image using the tracing of the first image as a guide, and make a second test strip. When all the negatives you intend to use have been treated in this way you can attempt a first print. It is vital that the printing paper is placed in the masking frame the same way each time so you must mark one corner of it, and of course after each exposure it must be placed in a light-tight box while the next negative is placed in the enlarger carrier. It is unlikely that the first print will be completely satisfactory since when more than one negative is printed on to a single piece of paper there will be a cumulative exposure which will result in the print being too dark in some areas, particularly where the two images overlap; in this case you can make a second print and shade these areas accordingly.

Another method of making a multiple image which can be carried out after the film has been processed is the slide sandwich. This involves placing two or more transparencies in contact with each other and making a print either from the combination or from a duplicate transparency. Unlike a double exposure in the camera a slide sandwich builds up density so it is best to select slides which are somewhat over-exposed. The technique tends to work best when one of the images is essentially light and fairly even in tone and the other is quite bold and clearly defined – a similar requirement in fact to a straightforward print montage – a silhouetted tree on a horizon, for example, could look quite effective when sandwiched with a high-key nude torso. Initially you will probably be able to find existing, possibly reject, slides from which to make suitable sandwiches but it can be more interesting and satisfying to plan your final image in advance and to shoot pictures specially for it.

When you want to produce images with an element of abstraction or fantasy a technique which has considerable potential is collage, in which separate images are cut out from prints made to size and pasted down to form a composite picture. Photographers like Bob Carlos Clarke have perfected this technique and combined it with other effects such as hand-colouring, air-brushing and toning to create quite bizarre and sometimes disturbing pictures.

As with a montage it is best to make an initial sketch of the final image after selecting or photographing the component pictures and then to use this to size up the individual negatives. Prints from the negatives should preferably be made on to a single-weight paper, and it is best to make two or three prints from each to allow for mistakes when cutting out. In most circumstances you will have a background image that extends over the whole picture area to which the others are added; this print should be dry-mounted. Using a pair of small, sharp scissors or a scalpel cut out each of the component images as close to the outline as possible and chamfer the back edge with fine sandpaper to reduce the amount the prints stands 'proud' when mounted down. Photo spray mountant is ideal for this purpose, and the edges of the prints should be rubbed down hard to ensure a neat join. Any imperfections can be retouched and the final collage rephotographed to provide a master negative. It is best to make the collage somewhat larger than the final prints are intended to be, and the reduction will also help to hide any imperfections.

Adding colour to black-and-white pictures can sometimes be more interesting and effective than shooting on colour film, and one of the simplest ways of doing this is by chemical toning. Most people are familiar with the old-

This montage (**top**) was formed by exposing two negatives on to the same piece of paper. Two identical negatives, one reversed left to right, were sandwiched together to create this symmetrical pattern (**above**). This texture screen (**right**) was produced by photographing a piece of mottled paper and using the negative in a sandwich with the image of the girl.

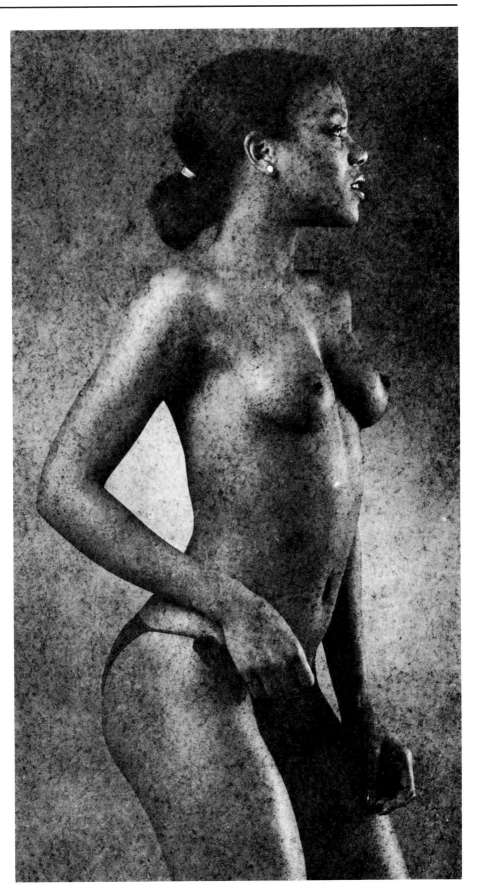

POST-CAMERA 3

fashioned sepia prints and this element can add considerable impact to the right photograph. There are many suitable toners available, some which require the print to be bleached first and then redeveloped, others which use a single solution. Any well-processed black-and-white print on bromide paper can be used; the process is carried out in normal light. In addition to sepia-toning, however, it is possible to obtain a wide range of colours in the image with the use of different solutions ranging from blue-green to red. As well as toning which adds colour to the darker tones of the print, leaving the whites unaffected, prints can be dyed, adding colour to the lighter tones but leaving the darker tones black. A quite dilute solution of ordinary fabric dyes can be used for this purpose; the print can be left in the dye bath until it takes on the required density of colour. There are a number of kits on the market such as the ColorVir in Britain which contain a variety of dyes and chemical toners which can be combined to create a wide variety of effects, in some cases with several colours on one print. This particular kit also contains a solution which produces a solarized effect; this can be used in conjunction with toners and dyes to give quite dramatic effects. By using a masking medium (obtainable from art supply stores) and applying it to certain areas of the print it is also possible to use the toning process selectively.

Another method of adding colour to a black-and-white print is by hand-colouring, where oil colours or water-colour dyes are applied directly on to the print with a brush. Unless you are particularly experienced with a brush then you may find the water-colour dyes easier to deal with, and resin-coated paper as opposed to fibre-based material can also be an advantage. As the dyes are transparent a full-toned print will tend to degrade the colours so it is best to make the prints fairly light and soft for hand-colouring, and some people prefer to work on a sepia-toned print. It is also a good idea to make two prints so that one can be used to test the colours before they are applied to the master print. You will need a selection of fine sable brushes and one or two broader brushes together with cotton-wool swabs and cotton buds, some sheets of fluffless, preferably photographic blotting paper, as well as the colours, a palette and a container for water. The print should be soaked in water first and the surface blotted dry before the colour is applied. It is best to start with the larger areas, mixing the dyes together on the palette until the right hue is achieved and adding water to dilute it to the right density. Large areas can be coloured either with a broad brush, a cotton bud or a cotton-wool swab. Blot the surplus dye from the surface of the print after each application. Use the finer brushes for the small details and when using the more concentrated colours, which should be left until last. Remember that the point of hand-colouring these days is to create an effect rather than to simulate colour film, and often the best examples of this technique are where the colour is added quite sparingly to selected areas of the print or to create deliberately unreal effects.

black-and-white print can be
sepia-toned to add a mellow,
old-fashioned quality to the
picture; this can be particularly
effective if the image has a
romantic style (**above**). Hand-
colouring is another method of
giving impact to a print. The
original picture (**far left**) was
sepia-toned and then the flower
was hand-coloured with
transparent water-colour dyes
(**left**).

INDEX AND ACKNOWLEDGEMENTS

ACKNOWLEDGEMENTS

All the photographs in the
book are by Jon Gray with the
exception of the following,
which were taken by Michael
Busselle:
8 (above), 9 (right), 16–17, 32
(above; below right), 34 (right,
above and below), 54, 58
(above), 59, 86–7, 90, 98, 100
(above), 102 (below), 104
(below), 106, 108–9, 110 (left
and below), 111, 114–15, 116,
117 (right), 118–19, 120 (below),
121, 122–3, 124–5, 128 (below),
129, 131 (above left), 142
(above), 144, 147, 148, 152, 155,
157, 158 (above and right), 159,
164–5, 166–7, 168, 170, 172–3,
174–5, 176, 178–83

Photographs by Jon Gray also
supplied courtesy of Tony Stone
Associates Ltd, London

Model index cards (30–1)
courtesy of Linda Lusardi and
Niki Clark

Photograph on p.138 courtesy
of Dunlop